trade
SECRETS
PETS

PETS

Katherine Lapworth

ORION

With grateful thanks to
the best kept 'trade secrets':
Jennie Sandford and Paul Woolf

First published in 1999 by Orion
An imprint of Orion Books Ltd
Orion House, 5 Upper St Martin's Lane
London WC2H 9EA

A CIP catalogue record for this book
is available from the British Library

ISBN 0-75281-825-2

Printed in Great Britain by
Clays Ltd, St Ives plc

Contents

Foreword

This was going to be a glowing introduction to the joys of owning a pet, whether of the furred or scaled variety. Instead, I find myself contemplating the lows as well as the highs of ownership while I scrape up the remains of whatever creature my cat has just deposited lovingly at my feet.

And yet despite these grisly hiccups, many of us find life unbearable without some sort of animal companionship. And what a wide variety of companions we choose. From stick insects to stallions, people surround themselves with all sorts of animals.

This book is intended to make living together a little easier. From making your dog smell sweeter with tomato ketchup to hypnotizing a rabbit, there are hints and tips for all animal lovers... and even a few to help you get rid of unwelcome pests.

'Man is the only animal that blushes.
  Or needs to.'
Mark Twain

'Women and elephants never forget
an injury.'
Saki

'But if you tame me, then we shall meet
each other. To me, you will be unique
in all the world.
  To you, I will be unique in all the world...
You will become responsible forever for what
you have tamed...'
Antoine de Saint-Exupéry

There is something in the unselfish and
self-sacrificing love of a brute which goes
directly to the heart of him who has had
frequent occasion to test the paltry
friendship and gossamer fidelity of
mere man.'
Edgar Allen Poe

BIRDS

....

'There was an old owl liv'd in an oak
The more he heard, the less he spoke;
The less he spoke, the more he heard
O, if men were all like that wise bird!'
Punch

Two's company

especially if you're out of the house a
lot. Two cock birds get on better than
two hens.

Canaries are not social birds

– they are quite happy to be kept on their
own. Two males will always fight as will
a male and female (except during the
nesting season obviously!).

What's the difference between the sexes?

Hens' plumage tends to be paler and not
as bright as the males'.

When choosing a bird, check it out for any signs of poor health.

It should have bright eyes with no
discharge and a good plump breast.
It should not have wheezy breathing,
a deformed bill or malformed claws.

Cock birds are usually easier to tame

and to teach to talk, and so make better
pets. Hens can be a bit destructive when
the breeding season starts.

Be careful when handling the plumage of a water bird.

It's a good idea to avoid touching it with your hands, especially if you're a bit sweaty. Wrap the bird in a clean cloth or bit of sacking to secure the wings.

To hold a small bird safely,

place your hand over the bird. Its neck should be between your first and second fingers; its wings should be safely tucked in the palm of your hand. Remember not to squeeze too hard!

Alternatively,

you can hold a small bird between your two hands but this isn't as effective as the first method if your bird is a biter.

Parrots make good pets

– and can be great mimics if taught from a young age. Mind you, they can also be extremely noisy and harbour vandalistic tendencies!

Make provision in your will for your parrot

– they often outlive their owners.

Budgerigars are popular pets
and can be kept inside or as aviary birds.

You can tell the sex of a budgie
by looking at the area above its beak
(called the *cere*); purple or blue means
it's a cock, brown means it's a hen.

Older budgies have a white iris
while younger birds (under 12 weeks)
don't. Young budgies also have fine black
bars on their foreheads which disappear
with their first moult.

Parakeets are quite happy in an aviary
and will often nest successfully.
Generally, they are better in a crowd
rather than as sole pets.

Cockatiels can learn to talk and whistle.
They make good pets because they're
usually cheerful and gentle birds.

Canaries are wonderful songsters
and live quite happily in an aviary
with other birds.

Finches enjoy the aviary life
but may need a bit of extra heating in the winter. Grow plants in and around the aviary to act as a windbreak.

Bengalese finches
make good foster parents.

Napoleon weavers are members of the finch family.
To encourage them to nest, grow bamboo in their aviary.

Mynah birds are quite hardy birds
but aren't keen on damp weather and so are happiest indoors.

Cages

Make sure the cage is large enough.
The bigger the cage, the better. By law, birds should be kept in cages that are wider than their wingspan.

Cage shape is important
- don't just go for a tall and narrow shape. For example, budgies should be kept in a space at least 12 × 24 × 24 in/ 30 × 60 × 60 cm.

Cockatiels are ground feeders in the wild
so spend a lot of time on the cage floor. It's better to keep them in a wide cage rather than a tall one (at least 14 in/ 35 cm square).

Square cages are better than round ones
- birds like the security of having a corner to hide in.

Bamboo cages may look pretty
but they are impossible to keep clean and some birds can peck them to bits in minutes. Go for a plain metal wire cage.

When you get a new metal wire cage
for your bird, wipe it down with vinegar and water to get rid of any excess zinc.

If your bird has a long tail,

make sure you have a tall cage to
accommodate its shape.

**When choosing a bird, decide what you want
from such a pet.**

If you want a pet to talk to and entertain
you, you will probably want to keep it
indoors so a cage is fine. If you want to
breed and show birds, you will need to
build an aviary.

If you're going to build an aviary,

think carefully about its position. It
should be located away from the road
so the birds won't be disturbed by noise,
passers-by or headlights. It should be
near the house where you can see it
but not so that it will disturb your
neighbours. Don't position an aviary
under trees or branches that could
damage the structure.

When building an aviary,

make sure the floor is easy to clean.
Concrete slabs or concrete are ideal.

Keep the cage away from draughts
or too much sunlight. Make sure
that other pets (such as cats, perhaps!)
can't get to it.

Get the perfect perch.
Don't just stick in a bit of dowelling
and be done with it. Birds need different
shapes and diameters of perch to exercise
their feet. Sticks such as bamboo or
willow that have varying diameter
are best.

Don't use cherry tree branches for perches
– they are toxic as are the resins in
unmilled pine. Most hardwoods (not
oak) and some fruitwoods (like apple)
are safe.

Natural perches
allow birds to chew on them which
is good for keeping beaks in tiptop
condition.

Never put sandpaper on the perch
because the particles can get stuck in
a bird's foot and cause infection.

African Grey's perches should be placed low enough
> to prevent the birds from looking down on people; it stops them behaving in an aggressive manner.

For greenery that looks good all year,
> chop up fake Christmas trees.

Put strips of willow bark
> in the nesting boxes of love birds.

It's easy to clean your bird's cage
> if you keep it lined with newspaper. Just take out each dirty sheet and replace it with a clean one.

Paper is the best medium to line the bottom of the cage
> because it is more difficult for bacteria to grow on it. It's also easy to keep an eye on the state of your bird's poo.

Never cover a parrot's cage with a towel or knitted blanket.

The bird might get its claws caught up in the material and end up hanging itself. Use an old sheet instead.

Birds will sleep better if their cages are covered.

During the day, it's a good idea to cover one corner of the cage so that the bird can retire there if it wants a rest.

Health and Cleanliness

Avoid accidents when clipping a bird's claws

– hold the bird up to the light so that you can see where the vein in the bird's claw ends and do not cut into it.

If a bird's egg is cracked,

a thin layer of clear nail varnish will preserve it.

If you're having difficulty getting your African Greys to nest,

place a pair of smaller, quieter, prolific birds in sight. Cockatiels and lovebirds are the best choice.

Spruce up your parrot

– spray him once a week with lukewarm water, first thing in the morning and before you clean the cage. A plant sprayer is ideal for this. Hold the sprayer so that the water drops from above onto the bird; never point it directly at him.

An African Grey parrot

benefits from a little rain and fresh air now and again.

If your parrot doesn't like being sprayed,

place a container of water in the cage and let him bathe when he feels like it.

Budgies are quite happy with a saucer of water

for their bathing requirements. Always clean out the saucer and replace the water; birds are like us, they won't bathe in dirty water!

Some breeders add a dash of raspberry cordial to their budgies' water

– they swear it kills bacteria and keeps their birds healthy.

The floor of a bird's cage must be cleaned each day.

Once a week, give the cage a good clean out (take your bird out first!).

You can change the colour of your canary

by adding paprika, cayenne or red pepper to its food.

If your parrot is feather-picking too much,

try a mixture of water and Aloe gel (1 tablespoon of Aloe gel to 2 pints/ 1.2 litres water). Spray the mixture onto him at bathtime.

Gaps in the wing feathers

of young birds and dried blood on the feather shafts of older birds can be signs of French moult which is a viral disease. Take your bird to the vet immediately.

To spot a sick bird
> look out for one with fluffed out feathers,
> closed eyes, dull and listless behaviour
> and a tendency to sleep a lot.

If you think your bird is sick
> turn the heating up. They can lose a lot
> of body heat when they're not feeling
> well.

Birds can deteriorate rapidly when ill.
> Contact your vet straightaway.

To examine a poorly bird,
> wrap him quite firmly in a warm towel.

Parrots need their beauty sleep
> – around 10–12 hours a night.

During the cold weather, make sure that there is enough humidity for your parrots.
> When the central heating goes on, the air
> gets drier. Place bowls of water near the
> cage.

Diet

....

Parrots grow tired of bird seed.

Spice up their diet with the occasional
hot chilli as a treat.

Fruit is ideal for birds.

The fruit shouldn't have any marks and
be washed thoroughly before being given
to the bird. Peel oranges and remove any
large pips or stones. Give your bird
a piece of fruit every day.

**Another good source of vitamins comes from
vegetables.**

Parrots go for cabbage leaves or stalks,
sprouting seeds (like alfalfa) and sprouts.
Freeze corn on the cob so you've got
some handy when it's out of season.

Food on the move.

Some birds, like softbills and finches,
rather enjoy eating live food. Mealworms
are the most popular but you could go
into cricket or locust production to
liven up your bird's diet.

Finches also enjoy
> finely chopped dandelions and spinach.

Budgerigars will tuck into the odd carrot now and again
> but be prepared for some orange stains around the bill.

Canaries will enjoy a bit of hard-boiled egg
> as well as canned corn. Small pieces of whole wheat bread are also greatly appreciated.

Cuttlefish bone is a good source of calcium.
> Position the bone so that the softer side is facing the bird.

Add a bit of variety to a parrot's diet.
> Bore a small hole in the top of hard dog chews and hang them up in the cage. Your parrot will find these fun to chew.

Parrots also enjoy seeds
> with a high oil content, such as cashews and peanuts.

Don't let your parrot out of its cage during mealtimes

– he may steal food from your plate which is annoying and he can get hold of food that is bad for him.

Collect berries in the autumn

and then freeze them to keep for treats all year round.

Millet is a great treat for birds

but be very sparing with it otherwise they'll end up eating it to the exclusion of everything else.

Birds need grit

to help them digest seeds.

Soak seeds in hot water

for 24 hours. This boosts the protein content and makes the seed easier for chicks or sick birds to eat.

Plastic containers are easy to keep clean

and are cheap; they will suit most birds. Parrots, however, need metal bowls.

Fresh water should always be available.
> Don't place the water beneath a perch.
> If your birds are in an aviary, check for
> ice during cold weather.

At Play

Keep them amused.
> If you've only got one bird, you could
> give it a mirror for company. They
> quite like listening to the radio too –
> the choice of station is up to you.

If your only bird is bored
> you could try introducing a mate.
> However, certain types of love bird won't
> accept a new mate after the old one dies.

A fir cone
> makes a cheap and effective toy.

Make a cheap playstand,
> fill a bucket with sand and stand some
> branches in it.

Parrots enjoy climbing hardwoods

like beech or ash. Scrub the wood with
soap to get off any dirt or parasites first.

Parrots like to dig

so place a pot filled with earth in their
cage and let them root around to their
heart's delight.

When you let your bird out to fly round the house,

make sure that you keep the toilet lid
down so he or she doesn't fly down
the loo.

Also,

cover any windows with an old bed
sheet. Large expanses of glass can
confuse birds and they could fly into
the window and stun themselves.

Cover up the fireplace too

– you don't want your bird disappearing
up the chimney.

Don't leave hot drinks around

while your bird is out of its cage.

Some plants are poisonous to birds
>so keep them out of the bird's way
>when it is flying around the house.

If you can't get your bird back into the cage,
>darken the room as much as you can
>because birds become more subdued
>in dark conditions.

Also,
>don't rush around after your bird. You
>can literally scare them to death. If you
>are approaching a bird, do so slowly and
>deliberately.

If you need to catch your bird,
>use a duster to carefully cover him
>before putting him back in his cage.

Some birds make great chatterboxes.
>If you want to teach your bird to talk,
>you will have to be patient – you won't
>get results overnight. Just keep repeating
>the lessons over and over again. Birds
>find it easier to mimic women's and
>children's voices. Keep the sentences
>short.

Cockatiels can be great screamers.

Sometimes this is because of boredom
or loneliness or because the owner
rewards the screaming with attention.
Don't get into bad habits. If your bird
is a screamer, try dropping a cover over
the cage when it starts. Remove the
cover as soon as the bird is quiet.

Racing Pigeons

To help make your pigeons go faster,

put them on the train when transporting
them. They much prefer it to the modern
day transporter.

Alternatively,

try something called 'widowhood'.
Separate the hen from the cock. During
the night, put them back together for
a short time. Then separate them again
and the cock should fly home faster to
be reunited with his mate!

To help get a ring on a pigeon,
>smear it (the ring, not the pigeon!) with
>petroleum jelly.

To buy food economically,
>get it directly from the farmer at harvest
>time.

To stop your bird's food getting wet in an outdoor aviary,
>place an old jam jar at an angle in a ball
>of cement and leave it to set. This makes
>a good sturdy feeder and the food will
>stay nice and dry.

To help the birds when they are moulting,
>feed them linseed as well as regular corn.

Protect your hen bird
>– watch that the cock bird doesn't punish
>her too much.

To keep the peace over the winter,
>separate the sexes.

To cut down on fighting,
make sure that the number of nesting
boxes corresponds to the number of
pairs. If there are too many boxes, some
pairs will use more than one and this
can start fights.

Chickens

Raising your own chickens means
you have your own supply of fresh
eggs and meat. Gardeners like them
because they keep pests and weeds
down and are a good source of
nitrogen-rich manure.

Choose the right breed for your purpose.
Some chickens are better layers
while others are better for eating.
Some, like Rhode Island Reds,
serve both purposes.

If you want your hens to lay eggs,
provide them with nesting boxes.
These should feel enclosed and secure.
A laying hen will produce an egg every
one or two days.

Try to keep your poultry yard in two halves.
The chickens can be kept in one half
while the grass grows in the other half.
Once there is enough grass there, the
chickens can be moved into the
second half.

Like other birds,
chickens need grit to help with digestion.

CATS

....

'The only mystery about the cat
is why it ever decided to become
a domestic animal.'
Mark Twain

'I love cats because I love my home
and after a while they become its
visible soul.'
Jean Cocteau

Cats are quite happy to spend time alone

so make good pets if you're out of the house for quite long stretches. They are also ideal if you live in a flat or busy city centre because they can adapt to living inside. They make good pets for people who can't get about too easily because they exercise themselves.

Female cats

are generally more affectionate and playful than male cats.

Once a male cat is neutered

it becomes less territorial and won't wander as far as a tom.

If you don't intend to breed from your cat

get it neutered. Female cats come into season several times a year so you'll stop unwanted pregnancies (and anti-social sexual behaviour in males). Female cats should be neutered when they're four or five months old while male cats should be done at six months.

Choose a pedigree cat

if you are intending to show or breed
from it. Like all pedigree animals, they
take a lot of time and money. Go to a
specialist breeder. If you are going to
show your cat, you will have to register
it with the correct cat authority.

Choose a moggy

if you just want a pet. They're cheaper
(often free) and usually friendlier than
the pedigree breeds.

Animal sanctuaries

are a good place to go to find a cat. Cats
are only there because they are lost or
unwanted.

Manx cats don't have tails

– just a hollow at the base of the spine,
but they do have very long hind legs
which give them great speed.

Always put elasticated collars on your cats
  – this will let them slip out of trouble.
  They are always getting caught up in
  things and a rigid collar can be
  dangerous.

Don't stare directly at a cat
  – it's interpreted as a hostile gesture.
  Scrunch your eyes up and blink slowly
  and you'll get on fine. Best of all, wear
  sunglasses. You'll look cool and cats
  love it.

It's a myth that cats should be put out at night
  – most moggies are happy to stay indoors
  and sleep.

Make sure your cat can sit at a window
  so he can see what's going on. Cats
  love watching the outside world.

A cat flap gives your cat freedom
  to come in and out of the house as he
  pleases. The best height to fit the cat
  flap is 6 in/15 cm from the floor.

Kittens

....

*'The trouble with a kitten is
THAT
Eventually it becomes a
CAT.'*
Ogden Nash

When choosing a kitten

watch its behaviour with its litter mates.
You will be able to get an idea of its
personality from the way it interacts with
the others.

When you bring your kitten home,

you should make it feel secure. Make it
a 'nest' out of a cardboard box. Wrap a
jumper round a hot water bottle and place
in the box. Put the kitten in for the night.

Check your kitten for signs of good health

before you take it home. Its rear end
should be free of diarrhoea or discharge.
Its ears should be clean and dry (excessive
scratching and dark wax could mean
mites). Its nose should be slightly moist
and feel velvety. The gums should be pink

and there shouldn't be any bad breath.
Check its coat for signs of fleas.

Kittens are more of a handful than adult cats

because of having to train them and keep
an eye on them. However, they're more
adaptable than older cats.

Mother cats teach kittens how to behave

(for example, how to use a litter tray).
So try not to separate them too early;
otherwise you'll have your hands full
trying to teach your kitten what it
should have learnt from its mother.

Don't separate kittens from their mothers

until they are fully weaned. This is
usually around eight weeks of age.

Take your kitten to a vet as soon as you can.

You will have to get it vaccinated against
Feline Entiritis and Feline Influenza (both
of which can be fatal).

When holding a kitten,

make sure you are supporting its
whole body.

When introducing your kitten to other pets
always be on hand to supervise the
meeting. If you already have a dog, keep
it on its lead or put your kitten in a
travelling case while they get used to
each other. Don't leave them alone until
they have got to know each other.

Health and Cleanliness

*'If toast always lands butter-side down, and
cats always land on their feet, what happens
if you strap toast on the back of a cat and
drop it?'*
Stephen Wright

*'There are two means of refuge from the
misery of life – music and cats.'*
Albert Schweitzer

Cats are naturally clean
so toilet training isn't too much of a
struggle. Start off with a litter tray; you
can use an old baking dish if you don't
want to buy a proper plastic one.

You can start to litter-train kittens
    from the age of four weeks.

If your cat keeps weeing in the same spot in the house,
    try feeding it in the same place.
    He'll soon stop using it as a toilet.

If your kitten has an bit of an accident,
    transfer the puddle or poo to the litter
    tray. This should attract the cat to it
    next time it wants to go.

Clean a litter tray at least twice a day
    – some cats are fastidious and don't
    like to use the tray if it isn't clean. Well,
    would you use the toilet if the chain
    hadn't been pulled?

If you're in a hurry,
    stack three clean litter trays on top of
    each other. You can simply lift off the
    top tray when it gets dirty and you have
    a clean one all ready and waiting to be
    used immediately.

Two cats?
Two litter trays.

If your cat doesn't take to the cat litter
try substituting it with soil.

Hooded litter trays are best
because cats prefer to pee up a wall
rather than into the hole they have just
dug.

Cats don't like having baths.
If you have to give your cat a bath
(because its fur has got contaminated or
you are going to be showing it) make sure
you have an extra pair of hands to help
you. Bathe it in a plastic bowl and use
a proper cat shampoo.

Cats should be bathed twice a year.
Put some cotton wool in his ears and
hold his front paws while washing him.
It's a good idea to get your cat used to
this when he is a kitten.

Cats have a routine when cleaning themselves:

first they clean the face and the top of the head with their paws, then they lick their shoulders, front legs and sides, finally they clean their tail.

Long-haired cats

need to be brushed and have knots and tangles removed each day. Cats with long hair are often more docile than their short-haired cousins.

Short-haired cats

don't need as much looking after as long-haired cats. They can groom themselves and it's easier to spot any problems, such as wounds, parasites and bad skin conditions.

A compromise between a long- and short-haired cat

is a semi-long hair. They have a long top coat and a thinner undercoat so are easier to look after than the full blown long hairs.

Get your cat used to being groomed.

Always brush him at the same time each day. It's usually best to do this after you have fed him.

Give your cat a glossy coat

by dabbing a cotton wool ball into some diluted vinegar and gently wiping it over his fur.

Alternatively,

use velvet, silk or a chamois leather for a bit of extra shine.

Protect your cat's paws when he goes outside

by rubbing in some hair conditioner.

Keep eyes and ears clean

by wiping carefully with a cotton bud dipped in warm water and a little baking soda.

A great way to groom your cat is by wearing a rubber glove.

They enjoy being stroked and you get rid of loose hairs while you are doing it.

To untangle knots in long-haired cats,
use a crochet hook.

Elderly cats find grooming difficult
so they need extra help from their
owners.

When grooming a cat's head or checking his ears,
put him in a pillow case or a terry
towelling bag with a draw pull so that
you can keep him in one place and you
don't get scratched. This is also useful
if you have to give him tablets.

If your cat suffers from a lot of hair balls,
rub some hair conditioner into his fur.
Check that it's not toxic in case your
cat tries to lick it off.

Cats are regularly sick.
It's the best way to get rid of fur balls.
Chewing grass helps them to throw up
with greater ease. So, for cats who don't
go outside, provide them with their own
bit of grass by growing it in a tray
indoors.

Alternatively,

other kinds of greenery do just as well as grass. Try thyme, sage, parsley or that old standby... catnip.

Cut cats' claws

with baby nail clippers.

Cats sleep for around 16 hours a day

so make sure they have somewhere comfortable to sleep.

A cat sleeping with its paws over its nose

was believed to indicate that gales were on their way.

Make sure your cat's food bowl is always clean

– cats are fussy eaters and won't eat from a dirty bowl.

If you have more than one cat,

make sure each has its own feeding bowl.

Tinned cat food contains all the right nutrients for a cat's balanced diet.

Now and again, you can treat them to fresh food: scrambled egg, chicken, meat, pasta, canned tuna or even porridge are often popular.

Feed your cat regularly

to discourage him from wandering from home and looking elsewhere for his meals.

Cats can never be vegetarians.

No matter what your beliefs are, cats need meat to survive.

Bad breath?

Fish may be a feline favourite but it causes a bit of stink afterwards.

If your cat refuses to eat,

try leaving his dish out with food in it but make sure it's just out of reach for a while. Cats can't resist thieving and this might be just the challenge they need to start them eating again.

Alternatively,

if you have two cats and one of them
isn't eating, feed the other one first. Cats
hate to be left out.

If your cat has lost his appetite,

try tempting him by heating his food for
a few seconds in the microwave. Being
natural hunters, cats prefer their food to
come at blood temperature.

Cat diarrhoea can be a problem.

A bit of cereal crumbled into his food
should help clear things up.

Dry food is an excellent diet for cats.

Test the quality of the dried food by
soaking a piece in water. The superior
brands, with a high meat content, will
only swell up a little bit.

Cats have a unique sense of taste.

They aren't any good at detecting
sweetness but they can detect the tiny
variations in the taste of water.

Administering pills can be a bit of a tussle.

Try wrapping the cat in a warm towel, keeping the paws and claws out of the way while you slip the medicine down his throat.

Alternatively,

crush the pill and mix it with some yoghurt. Put the solution into a pet syringe (available from your vet) and squirt it gently into the cat's mouth.

If getting medicine into the cat is proving a real struggle,

pinch his nostrils gently. He will have to open his mouth to breathe and you can then pop the pill in.

After a cat has swallowed a pill

it will usually lick its nose. If it doesn't, then be prepared for the pill to reappear!

Having a cat around can be a bit like having a child.

They can poke their nose into all sorts of dangerous situations so be aware of hazards. Don't leave small objects lying

around that can be swallowed, keep
plastic bags out of their reach, and don't
leave washing machine doors open.

Cats regularly get into fights with other cats.
Keep an eye out for bites and scratches;
they can become infected. If this
happens, try to bring the abscess to a
head by bathing it with salt water.

All cats have a third eyelid
which you shouldn't be able to see. If it
does become visible, it's usually because
your cat is unwell. Take it to the vet
immediately.

White cats get sunburnt easily.
On very hot days, try keeping them in
the shade.

Also be aware that the ears of white cats are prone to frostbite.

White cats are prone to deafness.

If a cat is affected by hypothermia,
> gently bathe the affected area in warm
> water. Then wrap the cat up in a towel
> and take him to the vet.

If your cat gets burnt,
> you must take him to the vet. You can
> help alleviate the pain by damping the
> scald with cold water (don't use butter).
> Hold an ice pack against the affected area
> and then put some petroleum jelly onto
> the wound to keep fur out of the area.

Unneutered toms are prone to leukemia.

Most dental problems can be avoided
> if you get your cat used to having his
> teeth cleaned regularly.

Excessive milk causes diarrhoea
> – cats are originally desert creatures and
> prefer water. If you do give them milk,
> make sure it's fresh.

If your cat gets cat flu,
> leave him in a steamy shower room for
> a short while to help his breathing.

You think your cat's got fleas?

If you find black grains of dirt in your pet's fur, take a grain and place it on a damp piece of toilet paper. If it turns red, it's flea droppings.

Get your cat used to his travelling basket

by placing his food in it for a while so that he gets used to the sensation of going inside.

Feeding your cat in her travelling basket

will make her associate it with nice things and not just vets and catteries.

Choose a top-loading cat basket

so your cat doesn't feel as if he's entering a long, dark tunnel. Make sure it has see-through sides for all-round vision.

To get rid of warts on your skin,

you could try this old wives' tale. Stroke the afflicted area with the tail of a tortoiseshell cat... but only in May.

Discipline

....

*'Women and cats will do as they please.
Men and dogs had better get used to it.'*
Robert Heinlein

Cats behaving badly?

Have a water pistol to hand. Then, if
they do something wrong, they get
soaked but don't associate you with the
punishment. If only men were so easy
to control!

Stop cats from using your lawn as a toilet

– sprinkle some pepper on the grass.
They hate the smell and won't go near it.

Keep cats off the lawn altogether

by placing litre bottles full of water
round the area you want to protect. Cats
don't like reflections and will steer clear
of them.

Orange and grapefruit peel
scattered round the garden will stop cats
coming in – they hate the smell of citrus
fruits.

To stop a cat scratching your furniture,
use lemon-scented polish.

Alternatively
rub citrus soap onto chairs and sofas.

Get cat hair off your furniture
by rubbing the fabric with a scouring pad.

If your cat claws your curtains,
dab a little peppermint oil onto the fabric
to warn them off.

**Prevent electricity and computer leads being
gnawed to bits**
– cover them with sturdy rubber tubing.
Just cut a section lengthwise and wrap it
round the wires you want to protect.

When moving out of a house,
put the cat in the bathroom or where no
one is likely to go. Put a sign on the door

to make sure it isn't opened accidentally
– otherwise, your cat will run off to get
away from the pandemonium of moving.

When moving to a new house,
keep your cat inside his new home for
at least a week. When you do let him out
for the first time, make sure he goes out
on an empty stomach so that he will
return home to be fed.

Prepare your cat for the arrival of a baby
– put baby powder and lotion on your
skin so that the smell becomes familiar.

If you have a new baby,
tie a string of noisy rattles across the
pram or cot. Not only will the noise alert
you if the cat jumps up but it will also
scare him and put him off trying it again.

To discipline your cat,
tap him on the nose, say 'No' in a loud
voice and then put him straight down
and ignore him. Cats crave affection and
respect, and will hate the cold shoulder.

Stop cats from climbing up vinyl wallpaper.
Keep a water spray to hand and give them a quick blast when they start their ascent.

Prevent cats from climbing over a fence
by spraying the wood with surgical spirit.

Also,
angle the top of the fence inwards so they can't get out of the garden so easily.

If your cat continually jumps onto kitchen work surfaces,
spray the surface with a little water and he will soon stop it.

If your cat continually chews your houseplants
spray them with diluted lemon juice.

Create an effective scratching post
– stick a carpet tile to a wall 2 ft/60 cm up from the floor. This should save your furniture from being reduced to shreds.

You can teach a cat to walk on a lead.

Start by getting your cat used to wearing a harness before attaching the lead to it. Practise walking around the house and garden before you try using the lead elsewhere.

Don't punish your cat if he brings home a dead bird or mouse.

He's only trying to contribute to the family; punishing him may indicate that you aren't satisfied with his offering and he'll go off and do it again. The best thing you can do is accept it gracefully and dispose of it as soon as possible.

At Play

....

'In ancient Egypt, cats were worshipped as gods. Cats have never forgotten this.'
Unknown

If you buy a cat

– buy two because they will amuse each other.

If you have two cats,
>don't separate them when they get into
>a fight. They have to learn to live with
>each other and they need to establish
>who is top cat.

It can take a month
>for two cats to get used to each other.

Cats enjoy playing.
>Try to give them at least 10 to 15
>minutes of your time each day.

Cats get bored with their toys easily.
>Have two or three to hand and keep
>rotating them every month or so.

Make your own catnip ball.
>Just cut the ends off a pair of old tights
>and fill with catnip. Double the tights
>over the ball several times and knot
>the end.

Make mazes out of cardboard boxes
>to amuse your cats. They love it.

Tortoiseshell cats

are usually female. On the rare occasion that a male tortoiseshell appears in a litter he is invariably sterile. But it's a myth that gingers are always toms.

Tortoiseshell cats are sometimes called

calico cats in Britain.

Read a cat's temperament by his tail and ears.

An upright tail and pert ears means he likes you. If the tip is slightly bent at the end, he's interested in what's happening.

If a cat's tail is wagging

vigorously from side to side or his ears lie flat then watch out!

A scared cat

will crouch down low with its tail held low and its fur all fluffed out.

A cat rubbing his body against an object

is marking his territory... and that can include you!

If your cat rolls over on his back and shows you his tummy

he is showing that he's completely at ease with you and trusts you. Don't try and tickle his tummy; cats are very sensitive there and you'll probably get clouted for your efforts.

A yawning cat is a happy cat

– even lions and other big cats do it to show each other that they are relaxed. Try yawning at your cat to let him know how much you enjoy his company.

Keep a cat happy for ages

– give him a cardboard box with a couple of holes in it. Brown paper bags are fun too.

CREEPY CRAWLIES

....

'Female moths are called myths.'
Old joke

Most insects are easier to handle if they're cool.
> Pop them in the fridge for a few minutes to slow their metabolism down.

If you have a wounded arthropod
> (that includes spiders, millipedes, centipedes, crustaceans, insects) with a damaged outer body casing, you can stick them back together with glue.

Spiders

....

'"Will you walk into my parlour?" said a spider to a fly:
'"'Tis the prettiest little parlour that ever you did spy."'
Mary Howitt

Tarantulas make great pets
> but they're not ideal to 'play' with. Enjoy the look of them rather than expecting them to play 'fetch'.

When buying a tarantula,

avoid one that is huddled up in the corner with its legs tucked underneath it. If it doesn't react quickly (or at all) to touch, don't buy it. It's probably dying.

A male tarantula will have little hooks on the undersides of its front legs.

Mature males live from a couple of months to two or three years, depending on the species. Adult females can live for decades; again, it depends on the species.

Different species of tarantulas need different living conditions.

Arboreals live in trees and make their homes in holes in the bark. Burrowers live in holes. You will need to reflect this when you design their cage.

Some tarantulas require very little attention

and are therefore easy to keep. Generally, the ground-dwelling tarantulas from arid climates are the easiest. Arboreals and spiders from wet regions need a lot more care. A good choice for the beginner is the Chilean rose tarantula.

A home for a tarantula

can be a 5 gallon/23 litre aquarium,
a large plastic jar, plastic shoe box or
custom-made cage. The top should be
covered with screen, mesh or cheese
cloth so that there is enough ventilation,
and secured tightly so that there are no
escapes.

Tarantulas are the Victor Meldrews

of the creepy crawly world; they don't
really enjoy company and are best kept
in solitary confinement.

Ground-dwelling tarantulas can easily be killed by a fall,

even a short one. So don't let them
climb too high.

Tarantulas love crickets.

Larger spiders will also eat baby mice
and bits of meat.

When a tarantula is about to moult

it will stop feeding, so remove food from the cage. For small spiders, this can be a few days; for adults, it can be up to several months before they moult.

Spiders that are upside down with their legs in the air

are almost certainly moulting. Just leave them to get on with it.

Don't feed a spider that has just moulted.

Leave it for a week until the new exoskeleton has hardened (usually when the fangs turn from white to black).

Tarantulas are venomous

– that doesn't mean that they are lethal, but bites from some species can be extremely painful and cause unpleasant symptoms. Some people can be allergic to the venom. If you are bitten and experience difficulty breathing, see a doctor.

Stick Insects

....

Always handle stick insects gently
   – their limbs are easily snapped in two.

Overcrowding can lead to cannibalism
   so give them enough space.

Make sure there is enough ventilation for your insects
   – damp conditions can harm eggs as well
   as adult insects.

Size is important when it comes to housing your stick insect;
   different species require more space than
   others. As a general rule, the height of
   the tank must be at least twice their
   length.

You can use newspaper to line the floor of your insect's home.

Some species, like the Giant Spiny, also like to rest on the floor so these will need a layer of peat to sit on or cork bark to hide under.

Sphagnum moss in the corner of the tank sprayed regularly

can keep the atmosphere humid.

A good temporary home

can be made from an empty sweet jar. Make sure you put some air holes in the lid.

Some stick insects need extra heat in order to thrive.

You can use a screened light bulb with a low wattage. A tungsten light bulb gives a very concentrated heat but make sure your insects don't dehydrate.

Stick insects are masters of camouflage

– some use shape and colour to blend into the background. Others will rock back and forward like leaves or twigs in a breeze.

Food isn't a problem

especially if you have access to bramble leaves throughout the year. Avoid leaves with brown edges or other insects eggs planted on the underside. Leave the leaves on the stem.

To keep food supplies fresh,

make a cut in the base of the stem and then set it in a heavy, narrow-necked water container (some stick insects are quite large and could knock over a container). Plug the top of the container with some cotton wool or tissue paper.

Try to vary the diet now and again.

The Javanese and Green stick insects are quite partial to rhododendron leaves. Some species will also take privet leaves, as well as rose leaves, oak and pyracantha.

Stick insects tend to prefer large leaves
> to smaller ones.

If you want to experiment with your insect's diet,
> do so after their moult when new food
> is more likely to be accepted.

Moults occur several times before the insect reaches adulthood.
> The higher the temperature, the greater
> the tendency for the insect to moult.
> Before a moult, your pet will become less
> active, even losing its appetite for a day
> or two.

Once a moult is complete,
> the insect will stay still for several
> hours while its 'new' skin hardens.
> Don't handle your pet during this stage.

Help your stick insect to exercise
> – put some dried twigs in his cage.

A rose by any other name...

some stick insects give off a chemical secretion that smells like rather pleasant perfume.

Don't let your stick insects escape into the wild

in case they manage to establish themselves. There are at least two species of New Zealand stick insects living wild in parts of south-west England.

If you want to encourage your stick insects to mate

take them on a car journey. Apparently this can arouse their romantic inclinations, especially those of the Giant Spiny Stick Insect!

Mantids are distant relatives of stick insects

but don't be tempted to keep them together. For many mantids, a stick insect is a tasty snack.

Unwelcome Visitors

'Nelson would have been afraid of ten thousand fleas, but a flea wouldn't be afraid of ten thousand Nelsons.'
Mark Twain

The most effective weapon against unwelcome creepy crawlies

is the vacuum cleaner. Use it regularly and make sure you always clean under the furniture.

Keep pests out of the shed and house

– spray insect repellent across the edge of the door and along the window-sill.

Wood lice like the damp.

Sprinkle talcum powder around the kitchen and bathroom floors to create dry surfaces. The wood lice will soon look for alternative accommodation.

Wood lice are also fond of house plants

– don't put plants out on window-sills and ledges; it will only encourage the wood lice to come into the house.

Get rid of book lice

– give them a good blast with a hair-drier on its hottest setting.

To prevent the spread of woodworm

treat wood in May. The woodworm larvae emerge in June and July so this should nip them in the bud.

Bed bugs love a cosy bed

so contrary to everything your mother told you, don't make the bed! Simply leave the bedclothes folded back down and the bugs will leave in search of a warmer home.

Sleep with your window open

at night to keep the temperature too cool for bed bugs.

If you suffer from asthma,

pop your pillow in the tumble-drier for 20 minutes on a hot setting to kill off any bed mites that might be lurking there.

Beetles and small flies often lay their eggs in flour and sugar.

Defy these disgusting breeding habits by always removing food substances from their paper packets and sealing them in airtight containers.

No fly spray?

Try hair spray instead. Flies hate it because it sticks their wings together – they'll soon get the message.

Avoid wearing too much yellow.

Flies love the colour and can mistake you for a large flower.

Midges and flies can be a real problem.

Cut a sock length off a pair of sheer tights and stretch over a baseball cap and down over your face for stylish protection!

Moth eggs won't survive intense heat.
If your clothes can stand it, give them
a quick tumble dry on a high setting.

Don't bother with mothballs
– just put some black pepper into the foot
of a nylon stocking and hang that in your
wardrobe.

Little spiders grow up...
into much bigger spiders. Plug up any
holes in outside walls, however tiny,
to stop the little ones crawling in.

Ants avoid any surface that has been treated
so try drawing a chalk line around the
area you want to protect.

Ants hate salt and pepper
so sprinkle a liberal dose to get rid
of them.

Alternatively,
use curry powder to get rid of ants.

If you're having a picnic and ants want to share the feast

> put a white piece of paper on the ground. The ants will make a beeline for that instead.

To stop ants going into your kitchen cupboards

> you don't have to buy pesticides. Just sprinkle some dried tansy around.

Aphids can wreck hanging baskets.

> Spray the baskets with soapy water to kill the aphids off.

Worms on a golf putting green needn't be a handicap

> – try spraying soapy water onto the turf. All the worms will come to the surface and you can simply remove them to a more convenient place.

Entice slugs from you drain

> – pour some turpentine down the drain. The slugs will come out and you can get rid of them permanently.

Alternatively,

put a piece of board or hardboard down
on the ground. The slugs will hide
underneath it to get out of the sun.
When you've got a fair crop, lift the
board up and wreak vengeance!

To make a slug trap,

bury a clean tuna can up to its neck in
the garden. Put some beer in the bottom
and leave it for the slugs to drop into.

Stop slugs from coming into the house

– try a line of salt across the doorway.
The slugs won't cross the line.

Stop slugs and snails in their tracks.

Smear petroleum jelly on the rim of
a flower pot to stop your plants getting
attacked.

Half a grapefruit

left upside down with the cut surface
on the ground makes a great slug trap.

Deter slugs

by scattering crushed eggshells around your tender plants. Slugs hate to crawl over such a rough surface.

Slug pubs

are a great bait. Cut slug-sized holes in the lid of a cottage cheese tub, fill it with beer and sink it into the ground. Slugs will be attracted to the beer and drown in it.

Keep flies away

– hang up bunches of elderflower.

If bees have taken up residence in your chimney,

light the fire. They'll soon leave and won't risk coming back (well, would you?).

After a bee sting,

crush some marigold petals on the affected area.

To soothe a bite or a sting,
   rub some fresh sage leaves on it.

Never swat a wasp.
   Many species give off a distress signal
   when swiped and, before you know it,
   you could be surrounded by his family
   and friends!

When a wasp lands on you,
   he's looking for something to eat. Keep
   very still and he'll soon realize that there
   is no lunch laid on, and he'll fly off.

Attract wasps with a jar filled with jam.
   Add some detergent and they'll drown
   more easily.

Mosquitoes hate Vitamin B
   so you could try eating copious amounts
   of vegetable extract spread (like Marmite)
   to stop them having a nibble of you.

Alternatively,

a pint of stout acts as a useful mosquito deterrent and is a pleasant way to keep them at bay.

Drive annoying insects away from you

on a summer's day; drink some tonic with a slice of lemon. The combination of quinine and citrus will put off most pests.

Insects hate the smell of

lemongrass, melissa, eucalyptus, tea tree or citronella oil. Use them when you're eating outside in the summer.

Catch lots of fleas in one go

– fill a hot water bottle with hot water, cover with double-sided sticky tape and then drag the bottle round the infected area. The fleas will jump onto the warm bottle and get stuck on the sticky tape.

DOGS

....

'There are three faithful friends – an old wife, an old dog and ready money.'
Benjamin Franklin

Having a dog takes commitment

– work out how much time you can
give a dog, where to exercise it and
how to get rid of its poo. What sort
of shape and size will suit your family?
Dogs cost money – the bigger the dog,
the more money! You should budget
for vet's bills, inoculations, food, and
possibly insurance and kennel fees.

When choosing the sex of your dog

remember that young unneutered
males can wreak havoc when they
go into sexual overdrive. Bitches go
on heat twice a year so need to be
watched carefully unless you don't
mind the inevitable attention of all
the neighbouring male dogs and
subsequent pregnancies!

Pedigree dogs

should be bought from a recognized
breeder. Like cars, pedigree dogs come
with documents that certify their
breeding and confirm their vaccination
records.

Cross breeds

are cheaper than pedigree dogs and are often less likely to inherit the diseases and ailments that pure pedigree dogs can suffer from.

Show dogs

require a lot of attention. They need to be groomed frequently and be incredibly well trained.

Working dogs

need a lot of exercise, and eat more than house dogs.

Lap dogs

need a lot of exercise because they are usually active breeds, but they won't eat you out of house and home

Guard dogs

give security and protection but you must be an experienced dog handler and know what the legal requirements are for owning such a dog.

A dog is the best security deterrent
   when it comes to protecting your house.

If you haven't got a dog,
   borrow a friend's and make a tape of
   occasional barks to play when you're
   away from home.

Trick thieves into thinking you have a dog
   by leaving a dog bowl outside, hanging
   a lead near a window or leaving the odd
   dog toy or chew around.

When fitting a dog with a collar
   you should be able to slip two fingers
   under it.

Put the dog bed
   in a busy part of your home, such as the
   kitchen. They enjoy being a part of the
   activity of the house.

When introducing a child to your dog
make sure they stroke the dog on its side,
not its front (dogs can interpret that as an
aggressive gesture). Dogs and children
should always be introduced to each
other in the presence of an adult.

Explain to children
that they must never rush up to a dog,
shout at it or pat it on its head.

Puppies

*'I loathe people who keep dogs. They are
cowards who haven't got the guts to bite
people themselves.'*
August Strindberg

Healthy puppies are happy to be picked up
and should feel firm and heavy.

Watch a puppy interact
with the rest of its litter; this should give
you a good idea as to its temperament.

When choosing a puppy,

check its ears – they should be pink
inside with no crusty or waxy discharge
(this indicates the presence of mites).

Also

look at its eyes; they should be clear and
bright, free from any discharge. If the
puppy keeps pawing at its eyes, this
could mean it has some sort of
inflammation or irritation.

A puppy's teeth and gums

should be pink (or black and pink) and
not smelly.

Check your puppy's skin

for oiliness or flakiness. There shouldn't
be any sores or lumps. If you run your
hand against the lie of the coat, you can
check for any parasites.

A puppy's bottom should be clean and dry

with no signs of discharge or diarrhoea.
If the puppy keeps dragging its bottom
along the floor it could mean it's got
blocked anal glands.

When you bring a puppy home,

check that there are no holes or gaps where he can escape. Pick up all small items that could be swallowed. Have the puppy's bed ready because he will be tired after all the excitement.

Make him feel secure

– this will be the first time he's away from his mother. A quiet spot, with a small pen that he can't escape from at night, is a good idea. Place a cardboard box inside, lined with an old jumper wrapped round a warm hot water bottle. Put a wad of newspaper nearby so he won't soil his bedding.

To keep a lonely puppy happy

– especially at night, leave a ticking clock nearby. It will be like the beating of his mother's heart so he'll feel more secure.

Decide where the puppy's toilet is going to be
in advance of his arrival. Take the puppy
there as often as possible. Look for signs
that he wants to go (whining, circling,
snuffling) and praise him to the skies
when he does it in the right place!
Don't punish him or rub his nose in
it if he makes a mistake – he won't
understand.

**Get your puppy used to being picked up and
carried.**
Don't pounce on him but reassure
him first before holding him firmly
but comfortably. Put one hand under
the puppy's chest and the other under
his rump.

Tag your dog
as soon as you get him home. More
and more vets have the facility to place
a microchip under the dog's skin.

Get your puppy used to wearing a collar.
Put his first collar on for short periods
each day. If you can't be around to keep
an eye on your puppy, remove the collar.

Puppies need to eat

three or four times a day. Once they are six months old, you can reduce that to two feeds a day. When they are between six and nine months old, they can go onto adult dog food.

A crate makes a safe and secure home for a puppy

especially if you keep it in a busy area of the home. It's somewhere for the dog to retreat to. Puppies are less likely to make a mess in their sleeping area so it helps when it comes to house-training.

Never leave a dog in a crate

for more than two or three hours a day.

A crate is for security

not for punishment. It's somewhere for your dog to want to go, not be afraid of.

Health and Cleanliness

....

'He that lieth down with dogs, shall rise up with fleas.'
Benjamin Franklin

'I think we are drawn to dogs because they are the uninhibited creatures we might be if we weren't certain we knew better.'
George Bird Evans

When your dog has rolled in something unpleasant,

wash him with tomato ketchup instead of shampoo. It gets rid of the strongest smells.

Prevent your dog from walking clumps of mud into the house

– keep his paws trimmed.

Incontinent dogs

can make your house smell awful. Put a bit of bicarbonate of soda in their drinking water to reduce the smell of their urine.

If your dog has a *wee* accident on the carpet

don't apply disinfectant; it reacts badly
with ammonia and could leave a mark.
Instead, try using a soda siphon and keep
blotting the stain until dry.

Alternatively,

dampen the stain with soda water,
sponge up the liquid and then let it dry.
Sprinkle on some baking soda and leave
for about quarter of an hour. Vacuum up
afterwards.

**Don't use products that contain ammonia to
clean up a dog's mess**

because it can remind a dog of the smell
of its own urine. If a dog can smell its
own odour, it will return to that spot and
use it again.

Long-coated dogs

need their hair brushing daily and should
have regular trims.

Smooth-coated dogs

are the easiest to look after and only
require a weekly brushing.

Curly coats

must be clipped every two months to keep them under control.

If your dog won't stand still while you groom him

put a yummy substance on the door of your fridge or oven and let your dog lick it off while you get him looking smart.

Use a non-slip mat to stand your dog on

while you groom him.

Grooming is a great opportunity

to check your dog for any parasites, sores, bumps and bruises.

A chamois leather

will bring out the shine on a smooth-coated dog.

Some long-haired dogs with silky coats don't have a downy undercoat

so need to be groomed carefully so that their skin isn't scratched.

Long-haired dogs should be groomed for at least 15 minutes

in order to keep their coats in good condition and looking tidy. Pay attention to particular areas such as under their legs (where hair can get matted), between the toes and on the hind legs.

Dogs with a wiry coat have to be 'hand stripped' every month;

you can pull the dead hair out with your fingers, always going in the direction of the hair's growth.

Some dogs have the kind of faces that trap dirt and debris

– the more wrinkly they are, the more they need keeping clean. Use damp cotton wool balls to clean out the folds of skin.

If your dog always jumps out of the tub at bathtime

leave his collar and lead on. Hook the lead over the taps. He will know he can't escape and bathtime will be less of a struggle for you both.

Stop your dog from scratching the bath

– put a nonslip mat down so that he can keep his grip and your bath is protected at the same time.

To protect your clothes when bathing your dog,

just put on a bin liner with three holes cut out for your arms and head.

Put dog shampoo in a squeezy bottle

and dilute with 50 per cent water. Just squirt it out and the thinner mixture will spread evenly through his coat, avoiding great clumps of bubbles that can be difficult to rinse out.

Use baby shampoo

if you don't have any dog shampoo.

Plug your dog's ears with cotton wool

when you give him a bath.

Avoid getting shampoo in your dog's eyes and mouth.

After his bath,
> dry your dog's head first. This is the first thing he'll shake so it saves you from getting soaked.

Give your gun dog a good rub down
> after a wet day's shooting. Use discarded newspapers instead of towels.

You can use a hair-drier to dry a wet dog
> but only if it has healthy skin. Heat tends to aggravate sensitive skin.

To dry your dog quickly
> use a chamois leather.

To get rid of fleas,
> start shampooing from both ends of your dog at the same time. The fleas get trapped in the middle and have nowhere to run to!

Discourage fleas
> with a dash of cider vinegar in the final rinse at bathtime.

Fleas hate garlic

so drop a garlic capsule into your dog's
feed to rid him of troublesome guests.

Alternatively,

add a couple of drops of tea tree oil to
some water and sponge your dog's coat.
This will get rid of fleas.

The best time to trim a dog's nails

is after his bath when they are softer
than normal. Don't cut into the pink area
of the nail because this is living tissue. If
you're not sure where to cut, ask your
vet to show you.

Over 75 per cent of dogs require dental attention

so keep your dog's teeth clean. Bad breath
is often the first sign of a problem.

It's tricky to clean your dogs teeth.

Make it easy by wrapping a fabric plaster
round one finger and dab on a bit of
bicarbonate of soda. Use your finger
as a toothbrush.

Don't buy expensive pooper scoopers

    – plastic bags over your hand work just
as well.

If your dog is in the habit of eating his own poo

    try and break his bad habit by sprinkling
his latest offering with a hot, peppery
sauce.

Train a puppy to relieve itself outdoors

    as soon as possible. Use the garden first,
where you can easily remove any mess,
before moving out to a suitable public
place where you can poop scoop away the
evidence.

Walking a dog helps to stimulate it to relieve itself.

    Always keep your dog on its lead until it
has done its business; then let it off its
lead to play. It will soon come to realize
that it has to poo before playing.

While your dog is relieving himself,
> say 'Hurry up'. As soon as he's finished,
> praise him. Your dog will soon start to
> relieve himself on your 'hurry up'.

If your dog suffers from incontinence,
> try fitting him with some disposable
> toddler training pants (with a hole cut
> in for his tail).

Alternatively,
> you could try giving him tap water that
> has been boiled and left to cool.

To get your dog to swallow a pill,
> cover the tablet with butter. Your dog
> will love the taste and the pill slips down
> easily.

If the dog won't take the pill this way,
> crush it up and mix it in some butter.
> Smear this onto his paws. He'll lick it
> off, taking the medicine with it.

Alternatively,
hide the pill in some cheese or put it in
some meat.

For dogs with a sweet tooth,
cover the pill with melted chocolate.

When giving a pill to a dog,
you should go to him rather than call
him to you.

To feed a sick dog,
treat him as you would a puppy. Give
him three or four small meals a day.

A good meal for a recuperating dog
or very young puppy is a bowl of lightly
scrambled eggs.

If your sick dog refuses to eat solid food,
try him with some gravy broth in a
saucer.

If your dog has an upset tummy,
feed him some bio yoghurt mixed with
a little honey to settle him.

If your dog hasn't eaten for 24 hours,
take him to the vet.

Spaying doesn't make a bitch fat
– eating too much food is the only reason
a dog gets too big.

If your dog needs to go on a diet
try to give him around 60 per cent of
his normal calorie intake.

Overweight dogs
benefit from increased daily exercise.

Dogs cannot live on meat alone
– make sure you vary their diet, mixing
meat with cereals, vegetables, pasta and
rice.

Dogs can eat their 'greens' as well as humans:
cabbage, potatoes and carrots are all part
of a well-balanced diet.

Want to go vegetarian?
It can be done, but talk to your vet about
getting the right balance at meal times.

Chicken is easy to digest
and much lower in calories than other
doggy meals.

Dried foods
have four times as many calories as
canned food so always serve in small
quantities. These foods shouldn't be
confused with dog biscuits, which are
mainly cereal.

For a high fat content,
try serving heart (it has double the
calories of kidney).

Always keep the water bowl clean
and refill it each day.

The best kind of feeding bowl
is made from stainless steel with a
bottom rimmed with rubber to stop it
from sliding all over the floor. Ceramic
bowls can get chipped and harbour
bacteria.

Don't treat your dog like a dustbin.
Giving him food he's not used to can lead
to stomach upsets. Stick to pet treats
instead.

Small dogs have small stomachs
so feed them small amounts twice a day.

Pregnant dogs
need to eat up to 50 per cent more food.

Old dogs should be fed
little and often.

Dogs' food should contain
protein for growth, fatty acids for a
healthy coat and carbohydrates for bulk
and bowel movements.

**Don't be tempted to substitute dog food with
cat food;**
it's too high in protein for a dog.

Pasta is a good carbohydrate source
but might need to be flavoured before
you serve it up.

Serve dog food

at room temperature.

If your dog hasn't eaten its canned or wet food after 15 minutes,

throw it away and give it a new serving at the next mealtime.

A low protein diet

can help an incontinent dog. Feed him with cooked chicken, fish and vegetables.

Gnawing on bones

is an ideal way to exercise jaw muscles and massage gums. Beef shin or knuckle bones are the best option because they are less likely to splinter.

Dog chews

have fewer calories than bones and are often a more convenient (and pleasant) alternative.

When your dog is teething and about to lose a tooth,

> give him an ice cube to chew. The tooth will fall out and the cold will ease any pain.

When travelling

> don't feed your dog just before a journey; you don't want to see the meal reappear!

During a long journey,

> stop every two to three hours to give your dog the chance to stretch his legs, relieve himself and have a drink.

A hot car – in summer or winter

> – can be a deathtrap. *Never* leave your dog unattended in warm weather or with the heater on.

Excessive panting and drooling

can be a sign that your dog is overheated. If this happens, move your dog at once to a cooler spot. Get rid of any excess saliva to help him breathe. Sponge his face with cool water before giving him a drink. If things look really bad, wrap him in a cool, wet towel.

For sea dogs (or any dogs that are travelling by water)

it's worth investing in a dog's life jacket. Dogs can swim, but can drown if they get exhausted.

Discipline

'When a dog bites a man that is not news, but when a man bites a dog that is news.'
John B Bogart

When training a puppy or new dog

use a long training lead for outdoors and a long light houseline for indoors.

Never use a lead to punish a dog.

Tone of voice is important
– dogs will learn to associate your tone of voice with their behaviour. He'll soon learn to know that your stern tone after he's done something wrong isn't much fun. Be clear about the signals you're giving him.

It's best to conduct training sessions
in quiet places, away from people if that's possible. You don't want your dog to be distracted while he's learning.

Try to finish your training sessions
on a positive note. Always encourage your dog.

After your dog has had a training session,
follow up the hard work with a bit of play.

Don't allow your dog to play with old shoes or clothes

because they'll assume it's OK for them to chew *any* shoe or item of clothing.

Enforce your training commands

with praise, physical reassurance and an immediate reward.

Gradually reduce the reward treats

as training progresses so that your dog reacts to your voice and body language rather than bribes.

Don't bother with a training session

if you or your dog are tired – it will just be a waste of time.

When using a choke chain,

keep your dog on your left side.

Never hit a dog across the nose

– instead, grab him on both sides of the head and growl at him. Mother dogs growl at their own offspring and it works a treat.

Don't force a puppy's training

– ten minutes at a time is about all they can take. Always make it fun for them.

Never train a well-fed puppy

– a full tummy means a sleepy mind and the puppy won't be able to concentrate on what he should be learning.

If your puppy has the habit of running off,

try hiding. Then call him to you. He won't be able to find you when he returns and it will worry him. He'll stay closer next time!

The first things a dog learns

are usually the commands 'sit' and 'come'. Start his training with him on the lead. Practice makes perfect.

To assert your authority

never let a dog go through the door before you. He must know who's boss.

If you are about to bring a new baby home,
> let the dog smell something of the baby's,
> like a blanket or vest.

Introduce your dog to the baby
> and not the other way round; you are
> introducing a new member to the 'pack'.
> Hold the baby on your lap and let your
> dog have a good smell.

When the baby is home,
> try to keep the dog's routine the same.
> Go for walks at the same time, feed him
> as normal and so on.

If your dog gets too excited when you get his lead,
> put the lead back where you keep it and
> sit down. After a couple of times, he
> won't get so excited.

Dogs that constantly pull on their lead
> are a nuisance. Try filling a tin with
> pebbles to rattle next to his ear every
> time he pulls… he'll soon learn.

If your dog is a bit bold or too fearful

fit him with a head halter. Then if he
pulls, his own momentum pulls the
head down and the jaw shut. This is
an alternative to a check chain.

A check chain is ideal

for bouncy dogs or ones with a rather
short attention span. Make sure you
don't put the collar on backwards
because this can cause discomfort when
it tightens. In the right position, the
chain only tightens when tension is
applied.

If your dog has to wear a muzzle,

make sure that he can open his jaw
and pant while the muzzle is on.

**Fights usually happen between dogs of the
same size, sex and age.**

When your dog meets another, keep the
lead fairly loose (a taut lead encourages
aggression) and praise him when he just
sniffs the other dog.

Reinforce a dog's respect for you
> by ensuring that your dog is never higher up than you are. Sofas and beds should always be out of bounds.

If your dog creeps up onto the sofa when he shouldn't,
> put a couple of whoopee cushions on the seat. The unexpected noise will deter him from doing it again.

If your dog steals food from kitchen surfaces,
> make a booby trap by tying a chicken carcass to a string of tin cans or similar noisy objects. When the dog steals the carcass, the shock of the noise that follows will soon teach him restraint.

Don't give in to begging;
> it can often become a habit with dogs, especially if they are bored. If you pander to their whims, you'll just reinforce the bad habit and end up with a fat dog.

Train your dog to always eat from his bowl
> which should be kept well away from where you and the family eat.

Incessant barking

can be hard to deal with. Squirt water in your dog's face whenever he barks and he'll soon stop.

To stop a small dog from yapping,

hold it up at arm's length and it will stop.

If your dog keeps digging holes in your lawn or flower beds,

fill a sock with pebbles. As your dog starts to dig, throw the sock out of an upstairs window so that it lands near to the dog – not on him! He won't know where it came from but will associate the unwelcome shock with digging and soon give it up.

If your dog starts to chew the furniture,

you can paint on anti-nail-biting fluid or oil of cloves to deter him. Better still, if you can catch him in the act, throw a cushion or something that makes a loud noise to startle him.

Also, stop your dog from chewing furniture
by rubbing vapour rub onto the places
where he chews. The smell lasts for
weeks and dogs hate it.

Catch your dog in the act
and then punish him. It's no good
punishing him a few minutes afterwards
because he won't realize what he's being
punished for and could just become
confused.

If your dog likes rummaging round the bins,
sprinkle the area with pepper to deter
him.

Make sure you keep the lids on bins
to deter your dog from having a poke
around.

Teach your dog to sit to command
with a small titbit. Hold the titbit
slightly below his line of vision and
command 'Sit'. He will sit down
automatically to get a better sight
of the food.

If your dog won't let go of the TV remote control

(or any other object), get up, ring the door bell and the dog should drop whatever he has in his mouth and run to the door. Grab the remote (or whatever) before he comes back.

Keep food treats by the door for visitors

to feed your dog if he's good and doesn't jump up at them when they enter the house.

If your dog keeps licking a wound

try rubbing vapour rub near the sore (not on it) to deter him.

A dog should obey you because you are in charge

not because he's frightened of you. Punishment is OK as long as it doesn't terrify or hurt the dog.

Don't call a dog over to you to be punished
because he will start to associate your
call with punishment. Always go over
to a dog to admonish him if he's done
something wrong.

If your dog doesn't like travelling in the car,
leave the engine running while you sit
with him in the back of the car and just
read the paper for a while. The dog will
soon learn to relax.

For dogs who suffer from travel sickness,
try children's travel sickness tablets.
Half for puppies and a whole one for
adult dogs.

Alternatively,
try sitting your dog on newspaper during
journeys.

Also,
sit the dog in a stationary car with the
windows slightly open. Then travel a
few yards so the dog gets used to the
movement. Do this regularly over a

fortnight, gradually increasing the speed and distance travelled until your dog is accustomed to the motion of the car.

If you don't have a car grille or special safety belt for dogs,

tie your dog's lead to the seatbelt anchor so that he can't move around too much while you're driving.

Sniffing the ground is a sign that a dog wants to relieve itself.

If you're in the throes of house-training, you will have a *very* short time to get the dog or puppy onto the newspaper that you should always have at hand.

Keep some of the soiled newspaper around

to show your dog or puppy so it can smell where it's been and this will encourage it to use the same spot again.

Don't punish a dog for making a mess in the house

– it will only make him more nervous and prone to more accidents.

At Play

....

'To his dog, every man is Napoleon. Hence the constant popularity of dogs.'
Aldous Huxley

'The more I see of men, the more I like dogs.'
Madame de Stael

Keep your dog occupied for hours
— make a hole in a rubber dog toy and fill it with dog treats.

Make your own chewy toy
— take a hollow bone, sterilize it and then fill it with cheese spread.

A bored dog can often indulge in destructive behaviour
so it's a good idea to channel his frustration into something such as playing tug of war. Make sure you always win though; you are the dominant one in

this partnership so don't start to play
until you've taught him to drop an object
on your command!

Train your dog to run to heel
so you both get a bit of exercise!

It is illegal to deny a blind person guided by a dog access
to any public place. These dogs are
usually better behaved than most people!

Labradors, golden retrievers and German shepherds
are the most popular breeds for guide
dogs. They are generally intelligent, hard
workers, large enough to fit a harness
and small enough to be controlled.

Hearing dogs are used to alert their owner to a variety of sounds,
such as the door bell, smoke alarms,
crying babies and so on.

FISH

....

'Do not tell fish stories where the people know you; but particularly, don't tell them where they know the fish.'

Mark Twain

Anglers

....

To put together a cheap kit,
remember to look through all the
magazines for second-hand equipment.

Avoid accidents.
Don't fish during a thunderstorm. Your
rod will probably be made from carbon
fibre which is an excellent conductor of
electricity.

**To keep your line free from knots when sea
fishing,**
simply punch a couple of holes high up
on either side of an ice-cream container.
Fill with water until it almost reaches
the holes. Place a small skewer through
the spool and place in the holes. As it
rotates, the line gets wet and you avoid
getting in a tangle.

To stop your canvas tackle bag getting wet,
always put it inside a heavy-duty plastic
bag when on the boat.

Stop your hook from corroding

by placing a few grains of rice in the hook box.

To extract a small lump of meat from a tin,

just poke in a straw. A little piece of meat will go up inside the straw. To get it out, just blow down the straw. The meat will be the perfect size and shape for bait.

It's important to keep your maggots warm in winter

so that they remain active and wriggly. If you glue polystyrene to the sides of their box they will keep warm and stay lively all day.

To add flavour to your maggots or luncheon meat,

sprinkle some curry powder on them the night before. The fish love the flavour.

Attract different sorts of fish

by dying your maggots with food colouring. For example, red maggots attract perch.

To encourage bream to bite,
> melt some molasses in hot water and
> then mix your groundbait into it. Bream
> have a sweet tooth and will love this.

When fishing for carp,
> try enticing them with luncheon meat,
> sweetcorn and potatoes.

Get rid of slugs
> – use them as bait for chub, dace, roach
> and rudd.

Freshwater catfish aren't fussy when it comes to bait
> – it seems anything goes. Anglers have
> been known to try soured clams, ripened
> chicken entrails, pig liver, coagulated
> blood and even bits of scented soap!

Try tempting a mullet
> with banana, bread, cheese, peas or pasta.

To stop your worms from sinking in the weeds
> when fishing in a lake, inject them with
> air and they'll float nearer the surface.

Don't harm the environment.

Keep your unwanted nylon and take it home with you. It's also a good idea to chop it up into pieces so if you do lose it there won't be too much damage done.

Protect your hands from the cold and wet

– rub them in petroleum jelly before you start fishing.

To keep your feet really warm,

wrap them in kitchen foil and then put a pair of thick socks over the top. Your feet will stay snug and dry all day.

Don't waste money on expensive moonboots.

Just buy your wellies one size too big and line them with some polystyrene.

To catch a really good salmon,

put an item of clothing belonging to your wife or girlfriend in with the bait feathers. Salmon respond to female pheromones.

Some brown trout are partial to...

other brown trout. You can tell a cannibal trout by its hooked lower jaw.

Rainbow trout in America have been known to reach 50 lb / 22.7 kg in weight;

unfortunately, they're a bit weedier in Europe with the maximum weight being around 24 lb/11 kg.

Waders will keep you dry...

up to the knees and thighs at least. Make sure your bottom stays dry too. Cut some rubber trousers off just below the knees and tuck them inside your waders. You won't look like a fashion plate but you will be more comfortable than your wet-bottomed friends.

Make sure you are safe when you go fly fishing.

Put a life jacket on, especially if you are wading because when you're in deep water waders can fill up very quickly.

Avoid falling into the water

when you are in a boat. Always remember to sit down!

Always be prepared for the big catch!

Take some black plastic bin liners with you and some bags of ice in a cool box.

When the big moment comes, put your
catch inside the bin liner and surround it
with ice bags. The one that didn't get
away will stay frozen for several hours
until you can get back to your freezer.

You are allowed to fish with a bow and arrow
on many American waters. The arrow is
tied to the end of the line and the reel is
fixed on the bow.

Fish Breeders

*'Fish say, they have their stream and pond;
But is there anything beyond?'*
Rupert Brooke

Imported fish can suffer from jet lag;
so it's not always a good idea to take
them straight home from the shop. A
good breeder will allow you to reserve
fish.

When choosing fish, check what size they will grow to.

You could end up with a very large fish in a very small aquarium! Piranhas can grow up to 12 in/30 cm long while some Angelfishes can reach 16 in/40 cm.

If you've never kept fish before,

start off with freshwater species rather than the more demanding marine fishes. Tropical freshwater fishes can be just as colourful and attractive to look at as their marine counterparts.

Coldwater freshwater systems

don't need as many bits of technology as the tropical systems but they are more difficult to maintain. Coldwater fish consume more oxygen than tropical fish; therefore you will need a larger tank with aquatic plants to oxygenate the water.

Tropical marine fish are more expensive

than freshwater ones so it's worth getting a bit of experience with other (cheaper) fish before you move into this area.

Some fish need more expert care and handling than others;

for example, the moray eel, sea horses and the venomous lailbar Lionfish are really only for the more experienced fish keeper.

Make sure your fish will get along together.

Some fish can't stand the company of their own species but will happily share a tank with others. This might be a bit obvious but don't put carnivorous fish into an aquarium with small fish... you might start to notice that numbers are dwindling. Carnivorous fish should be kept on their own or with fish of a similar size to themselves.

A mix of species is a good idea

because different fish tend to have different habits, live in different parts of the aquarium and move around during different parts of the day. For example, catfish feed at the bottom of a tank while tetras move happily around all areas.

Koi and goldfish can live for over 20 years
> while killifish only last for a year.
> A good rule of thumb is: the larger the
> fish, the longer it will live.

When transporting koi in a car,
> make sure the fish is in a container that
> doesn't allow it to turn round. Then
> place the container so that the fish is
> lying across the car and not back to front.
> This stops the fish from banging his nose
> every time you brake.

When transporting very small fish,
> twist the corners of the plastic bag and
> secure with an elastic band. This stops
> the fish from getting crushed in the
> corners.

When bringing new fish home,
> put their plastic bags or containers inside
> brown paper bags. This stops them from
> getting too stressed on the journey.

You don't need to buy a net
> for catching fish in an aquarium; a plastic
> bag will do just as well.

Health

....

If you want to dispose of a terminally ill fish,
don't flush it down the loo. Fish can
survive for some time in the warm water
of the sewers. The humane way is to put
water in a jam jar, put the fish in the jar
and place in the freezer.

A healthy fish
should always have an erect dorsal fin.

A healthy fish should also have
a good strong colour with no blurring and
it should be eating regularly.

An unhealthy fish
can swim with its fins held flat against
its body. Avoid fish covered in spots,
lumps, wounds or split fins. Don't buy
a fish if the tank contains dead fish.

If your male fish refuses to mate,
make him jealous. Introduce a bit of
competition by making a false fish out

of paper. Wriggle it about in the tank
for a while. It should hopefully make
your male get his act together.

To encourage egg laying,
cut nylon wool into 18 in/45 cm strips.
Tie one end around a stone at the bottom
of the tank then secure the other end to
a piece of cork so that it floats. Your fish
will lay their eggs along the small pieces
of wool.

A great way to catch flies for your fish
is to attach a piece of fine net to the side
of your car in the summer.

To feed your fish using a timer
drill three holes into a clock face at
the times you want the fish to be fed.
Remove the minute hand and place
some food over the holes. Suspend the
clock face over the tank. When it's
dinner time, the big hand will knock
the food into the tank.

Fishy food treats
are pieces of cucumber, lettuce,
crumbled cheese, tinned peas or orange.
Chop them up into fish-bite size.

Don't overfeed your fish.
They should be able to have finished
dining within two minutes. Anything
left over just mucks up the water.

Feed fish little and often.
Like all animals, fish thrive on a
balanced diet.

Nominate one member of the family as the fish feeder
or have set feeding times so you don't
run the risk of the whole family dropping
meals into the water and overfeeding the
fish.

Grow your own whiteworms.
Buy a few to start off with from a fish
dealer. Put the worms in a box of earth
and cover with a slice of wet bread. This
should give you a continuous supply of
worms for your fish.

A good way to hatch brine shrimp

is to place them in an empty milk bottle.

Feeding fish with fresh fish

is nutritionally very good for them.
Always feed freshwater fish to salt water
fish and vice versa.

To stop big fish eating small eggs,

put some net curtain or glass marbles at
the bottom of the tank. The eggs will drop
between the holes and cracks to safety.

To feed fry fish

(and stop the bigger fish from getting
more than their share), use a gravy baster
to squirt the fry food in the right
direction.

Aquariums and Tanks

....

Don't overcrowd your aquarium.

You should keep three fish for every
2 gallons/9 litres of water. If you've got
more fish than that, you will need to get
an air pump.

A tropical freshwater aquarium
should be kept at a temperature of
around 25° C /77° F.

**Don't tip your new fish into their aquarium
straight away.**
You have to let the temperature of the
water in the carry bag equalize with that
of the aquarium water. The easiest
solution is to float the bag in the tank for
a couple of hours before netting the fish
into the water.

**If you are planning to introduce new fish to an
established tank,**
keep them in quarantine for a couple
of weeks. Quarantine expensive fish for
longer (at least a couple of months).

When you set up a new aquarium,
let it 'settle' for at least a week before
you start introducing fish. And then, the
first fish to go in should just be a couple
of goldfish. If something's wrong with
the tank and the fish die, you won't have
wasted lots of money on expensive fish.

When setting up a new tank,

use the filter from an old tank to
establish beneficial bacteria into the new
water immediately.

Rainwater is ideal for aquariums

but not if it comes from a dirty roof or
metal containers.

Think carefully about where you are going to place your aquarium.

Try not to put it in a window; the sun
can cause too much algae to grow and
the water to overheat. You need to be
near an electrical point to run the filter,
air pumps and heaters.

You will need a heater if you intend to keep tropical fish.

Allow 10 watts of power per 9 pints/
5 litres of water for a tank that is in
a normally heated room. If you have a
large tank (over 36 in/90 cm long), install
two heaters.

If you have to take your fish out of the water,
place it on a baby changing mat. The
raised edges will stop it sliding off. Also,
cover the fish with a soft, damp cloth.

**Filling your tank with plants and rocks makes
it look more attractive**
but don't go overboard. Your main aim
is to copy the natural habitat of the fish.

Rocks in tanks shouldn't contain calcium
– test them by dabbing them with a bit
of vinegar. If they fizz, don't put them in
the tank.

For fish that like caves,
use terracotta plant pots in tanks. They
make great breeding grounds.

A good alternative plant fertilizer for tanks
is rabbit or guinea pig droppings. They
won't harm the fish and they do a lot
for the plants.

If your fish like alkaline conditions,
> sprinkle a bit of baking powder into the
> water.

For fish that like more acidic water,
> put a tea bag in the tank. This will also
> encourage plants to grow.

Plants are a good way of absorbing carbon dioxide and producing oxygen;
> they also remove nitrate from the water,
> while some plants are part of a fish's diet.

Plants are also an ideal way of hiding the technical bits and pieces
> that you need to run your aquarium.

When planting up your aquarium,
> put the taller plants at the back but
> don't position them too close together.
> The odd gap here and there will give
> an illusion of distance and space.

You can't keep live plants in a marine aquarium

but you can use synthetic plants and corals to liven things up.

Purify the water in a tank

by putting watercress in the filter chamber. Buy it ready-prepared from a supermarket or grocers. If you introduce it from the wild, you run the risk of introducing diseases into the water.

Stop fish from getting cold during a power cut,

place a plastic bottle filled with hot water inside their tank. Replace it as necessary.

When cleaning out your fish tank,

don't throw away the water. Put it on your garden instead. It's full of nitrates which will do your plants a lot of good.

To clean a tank,

remove one third of the water every fortnight, replacing it with clean water.

Bring out the exotic colours of your fish
by exchanging the gravel in your tank
with coal.

Get fish used to shows
– place their tank in a busy part of the
house.

**To make male fish display themselves
effectively for competitions,**
place them in adjacent tanks so they can
show off to each other.

Ponds

**Remove blanket weed from the side of a
pond,**
use a windscreen ice scraper.

If you're planning to build a fish pond,
don't make it too involved. Awkward
shapes can cause water to stagnate in odd
nooks and crannies.

Don't situate your pond underneath trees

because you'll have your hands full
keeping the surface clear of falling
leaves.

During a frost,

make sure you leave an air hole for
your fish to breathe. Float a rubber ball
on the surface overnight. During the
day, you can take the ball away and,
if possible, draw off some of the water
so that oxygen can reach the surface.
Never break the ice with a hammer –
it's like a bomb going off at close quarters
and the shock waves can kill the fish.

If you've forgotten to leave an air hole,

heat a pan of water and hold it on top
of the ice so that it melts through leaving
a perfect hole.

HORSES

....

'Four things greater than all things are –
Women and Horses and Power and War.'
Rudyard Kipling

Horses are sensitive souls

so don't shout at them. Tone of voice is important. Speak calmly and with authority.

And they have sensitive spots...

well, ticklish ones anyway. Be careful around the stomach, flanks and inside thighs.

Always warn a horse if you are going to walk behind him.

Horses don't like surprises. Run your hand along his back and quarters as you move behind him so he knows where you are all the time. You're harder to kick if you're close.

Keep an eye on the ears.

They are a good barometer of mood. Pricked forward, they mean that a horse is alert. Ears back could mean the horse has heard something behind him or that he's unhappy about something. Ears flattened back is a sure sign of anger.

Signs of distress
(due to fear or pain) are showing the
whites of the eyes, snorting a lot,
sweating and increased breathing.

Horses are creatures of habit;
they love routine. So make sure you
feed, clean and exercise them regularly.

**A 'cob' horse is known for its dependability
and strength.**

When buying a horse,
ask the owner to ride it first and
then get a friend to ride it for you.
You can then see what its action and
temperament are like before you have
a go yourself.

When trying out a new pony to buy
the people who are selling often ride it
away from the house or stables and let
you try riding it back. Instead, ask to
ride it away yourself; if it swishes its tail
or is stubborn, you know it's likely to be
trouble.

Always ask to see a horse being ridden in traffic before you buy.

A traffic-shy horse can be a liability if you enjoy hacking out. Don't try to ride a strange horse yourself in traffic.

When tacking up, talk to your horse.

Approach him so he can see you and keep talking to him to reassure him.

To check that the stirrups are at the right length,

adjust the leathers so that your fingertips rest on the stirrup bar and the base of the stirrup reaches your armpit.

To check the length of the stirrup leathers once you are on the horse,

ensure that the base of the stirrup reaches your ankles when you let your leg dangle down.

When you are about to mount,

make sure the horse is standing still and squarely. You don't want to catch him or yourself off balance.

As you mount your horse, try to avoid digging your toes into his side.

> This will only make him move away from you and it will be harder to mount properly.

Don't frighten your horse by throwing a whole rug over him,

> fold the rug in half before placing it over the horse and then gently unfold it once it's on his back.

If loud speakers or low-flying planes distract your horse,

> just put a little cotton wool in both his hears, being careful not to push it too far down.

When turning your horse,

> make sure you haven't gone so far into a corner that his hind quarters can't follow properly.

When riding, keep your shoulders parallel with your horse's shoulders.

When trotting,

> your hands should remain still and you
> should absorb the rise and fall motion
> through the ankle, knees and hips. Lean
> slightly forward and stay relaxed.

**If you are going out in the country for a ride
for the first time,**

> plan your route carefully in advance.
> Let someone know that you are going
> out, what your route is and what time
> you plan to return.

When riding out in the countryside

> if in doubt, walk. Keep an eye open for
> potential hazards like boggy ground,
> low branches or slippery surfaces.

As you ride uphill,

> lean forward and let your horse stretch
> his neck out. This allows your horse
> to use his hind quarters and legs more
> effectively.

Always *walk* through water

> unless it is very shallow. Galloping at
> full tilt through water may look great on

the movies but you want to be sure that the footing is safe and secure for both you and your horse.

Clothes and Equipment

Don't make your saddle too slippery
when polishing it; clean the straps and underneath but never the top part where you actually sit or you could come a cropper.

Don't saddle soap the seat of your saddle
(try saying that quickly after a few drinks!) or you'll end up with a black bottom.

To stop your saddle from drying out,
try putting some hair conditioner on it. Rub it in as you would polish.

Put oil on your tack
to make is soft and supple – especially when new.

Don't wear one stirrup out faster than the other.

Although you always mount from the left, you can cut down wear on stirrups by swapping them round every couple of weeks.

Always run up both stirrup irons after dismounting.

This avoids them hitting the horse when he moves and it's easier for you to carry the saddle this way.

If you have to leave a horse when you've tacked up, loop the reins under the stirrups

so that they don't get in the way.

Saddle racks can quickly mark saddles

so glue a couple of pieces of foam onto the racks to protect expensive tack.

Make saddle soap go further

– melt it down in some milk before using.

Soak a new pair of boots

in manure overnight. It will draw out
any excess grease and they'll stay easier
to clean.

Get a great shine on your boots

without too much elbow grease. Polish
them with washing-up liquid and leave
overnight.

Alternatively,

furniture polish will shine boots. For
extra sparkle, try a final rub down with
some nylon tights.

For a really rich shine

on boots, the penultimate layer of polish
on black boots should be brown.

To harden up new boots,

add a few drops of methylated spirits
to the water when first cleaning.

Tight-fitting boots can be hard to pull on.

Wear a pair of pop socks over the tops of
your jodhpurs and the boots should slip
on more easily.

To keep boots in pristine condition
> don't go to the expense of buying inner woods. Old nut bags scrunched up inside a soft pillow case and stuffed inside the boots will work just as well.

Keep your grip when riding
> – don't polish the inside of your boots.

Also,
> for extra grip, wear jodphurs with suede bottoms or chaps.

Avoid unnecessary discomfort when riding
> – don't wear skimpy underwear which can rub. Really big pants may not feel glamorous but they will be far more comfortable and won't show under tight-fitting jodhpurs either.

Buff up your velvet hat
> by leaving it in the bathroom when you take a hot, steamy shower.

When learning to ride, wear fitted clothing
> so your teacher can see your position and correct it if necessary.

Keep your hoof pick clean
– just ask your vet for an old syringe holder to keep it in.

To prevent your hoof pick from disappearing,
tie some bailer twine to it. That way, if you do drop it in the straw, you can retrieve it easily.

To stop your horse from becoming cast
(stuck against the wall), always bed him down with big bails of straw.

To skip out,
you don't really need an expensive shovel and broom. The side of your foot and an old washing basket is just as good.

Soak hay overnight
in a wheelie bin. Just pierce a hole or two in the bottom to let the water drain out. Once soaked, it will be much easier to move the hay around.

Always tie haynets up high
so your horse won't get tangled in them.

To open a bale of hay or straw, use another piece of twine to cut it open.

Slip the piece of twine under where you want to cut and then saw it backwards and forwards. The twine holding the hay together will always come apart first.

Horse Care

....

Try not to throttle your horse!

When fitting the bridle, put your hand underneath the throat-leash to check that there is enough room to allow him to breathe.

When washing greys,

for that whiter than white tail, use a blue rinse shampoo.

To make your horse's features stand out,

rub a little Vaseline round his muzzle and eyes.

Plaiting a mane can be difficult
> but a little hair gel rubbed through before you start will make all the difference.

Alternatively,
> use some egg white to keep the flowing locks under control.

When plaiting your horse's tail before travelling,
> cut one leg off some tights and stretch it over the plait to stop it falling out.

For showing, set the mane to one side
> of your horse's neck with a little egg white.

To get a horse's mane to lie over
> comb it the way you want it to lie and then dampen it down every day.

When pulling a mane,
> a little oil of cloves rubbed into the hair will help to prevent tangles.

To keep a horse's tail shiny and tangle-free
   put a little baby oil in some water and
   spray onto the tail. Run your fingers
   through to the tips.

Alternatively,
   washing it with some fabric conditioner
   works wonders!

Also, if his tail is in a tangle,
   comb some hair conditioner through it
   to get rid of the knots.

To take the sweat off a horse,
   try winding some bail twine around your
   hand; it makes a great scraper and you'll
   be able to get into all the curves of a
   horse's body.

If your horse or pony lives out during the winter, don't groom him.
   The mud that they get themselves
   covered in acts as a second coat and
   insulates them against the cold.
   They may look scruffy but they'll
   be warm too.

If your horse gets really greasy,

he can be difficult to clean. Dip a towel in some methylated spirits and hot water and wipe over; this will draw the grease from his coat.

If you need to get your horse *looking* clean in a hurry,

damp a cloth (an old dishcloth will do) and wipe it over his coat to produce a clean-looking shine.

Keep two sponges handy for cleaning your horse:

one for the eyes, nose and mouth area and the other for the dock area. It's a good idea to have them in different colours so you don't confuse the two.

To give a shine to a horse's hooves

rub in some hair conditioner.

When a foal is first born,

push the mane neatly to one side while it is still damp and it will stay like that.

To calm a young foal,
scratch his neck.

If your foal won't suckle,
try tickling his bottom; it stimulates
the sucking reflex.

Strengthen your horse's shoulder muscles
by holding a carrot to one side of his
head, let him take a bite and then move
the carrot to the other side. Make sure
you exercise each side equally.

**You can use a carrot to strengthen a horse's
legs.**
Place the carrot between his front and
back legs and he will reach down to eat
it. Again, always make sure you repeat
this exercise equally on each side of the
horse.

Pick your horse's feet out at least twice a day
and after exercise. Horses should be shod
every four to six weeks.

Never dice carrots

– always chop them lengthwise;
otherwise you run the risk of your horse
choking.

Feed little and often.

Horses have small stomachs, digest
food slowly and can't take a huge meal
in one go.

Don't feed a horse

if he is hot and tired.

When feeding a horse titbits,

keep your hand flat. You don't want your
fingers to become part of the snack.

To make bran mash,

put 2–3 lb/900–1350g of bran in a bucket
and pour boiling water over it. Stir,
adding a handful of salt and a handful
of oats. Place a sack over the bucket
and let the mixture steep until it is cool.
You can add chopped carrots and apples
as an extra treat.

If you must change your horse's diet,
    do it gradually. Horses don't like sudden
    changes and it could lead to colic.

For fussy feeders,
    add molasses to the feed.

After exercising during the winter,
    give your horse warm water to drink
    rather than straight from the tap. Cold
    water could give him colic.

Never feed or water a horse straight before or after heavy work
    – you could give him colic.

If your horse is allergic to dust or spores,
    use shredded paper as bedding rather
    than sawdust, straw, shavings or peat.

If your horse is difficult to catch,
    always approach him from a 45° angle;
    it's much less threatening than head on.

Mounting a horse
can be tricky if you've had a hip
placement or are arthritic. Always try
to use a mounting block.

Help children to look up when jumping.
Stand the other side of the jump and ask
them to shout out how many fingers
you're holding up.

**Persuade children to keep their hands up
while they're in the saddle**
– ask them to hold a cup of water or a
tray of drinks and see how much they
spill (don't use your best crystal for this!).

**Teach children to relax and breathe while
they're riding**
– encourage them to sing a song when
doing rising trotting.

Try looking a gift horse in the mouth.
You can tell the age of a horse by looking
at his teeth. The more angular they are,
the older the horse is.

A piggy eye,
> where too much white is showing, is
> often thought to indicate a mean nature.

Donkeys

....

*'I believe I would rather ride a donkey than
any beast in the world. He goes briskly, he
puts on no airs, he is docile, though
opinionated. Satan himself could not scare
him, and he is convenient – very convenient.'*
Mark Twain

Donkeys have a strong sense of self-preservation;
> if they think something is dangerous,
> they won't do it... so don't make them!

Like horses, donkeys are sociable creatures
> – it's best to keep them with another
> donkey or horse.

Donkeys are originally desert creatures
so don't handle the cold as well as some
other animals. Make sure they have
adequate shelter.

A dirty donkey is a happy donkey.
They use dust and grit like a shampoo
to keep their coats in good condition.

Donkeys can live to a ripe old age,
sometimes over 40 years, so they are
a long-term commitment.

RABBITS AND GUINEA PIGS

....

'Master Rabbit I saw'
Walter de la Mare

Rabbits

....

*'The rabbit has a charming face,
It's private life is a disgrace.'*
Anon

Cool your rabbit down in summer.

Chill a ceramic tile in the fridge and then
place it in his hutch.

Use sawdust on the floor of the cage

rather than wood shavings or straw.
Sawdust is softer and more comfortable.

The bigger the cage the better.

It should be at least four times the size
of the rabbit and a lot more if he's going
to be confined for most of the day.

Rabbits come in different sizes.

For example, Netherland Dwarf rabbits
are tiny (weighing in at 2¼ lb/1 kg) while
the Belgian Hare (which isn't a hare but a
rabbit just to be confusing!) can weigh up
to 9 lb/4 kg.

Hang a carrot from the cage using a metal skewer.

It will stay fresh longer and remain free from sawdust so your rabbit will enjoy it more.

Amuse a house rabbit

– tell it some jokes... no, seriously, put its food in a washing ball. This keeps it happy for hours.

Paper bags and cardboard boxes

make great places to hide. Rabbits also have fun playing with cardboard loo rolls, bits of paper to shred, small towels, things to jump on and hide under.

Keep an eye on a rabbit when it's loose in the house.

Rabbits are great chewers and think nothing of sinking their teeth into electric cables, rugs, plants and so on.

You can train a house rabbit to walk on a harness and lead.

But don't take them for long walks in unfamiliar territory. Stick to the familiar.

Prepare a crunchy snack
by baking left-over bits of bread.

Always make sure your pet has enough water.
If you keep the hutch outside, remember
that the water in its bottle can freeze in
the winter so don't fill it right to the top
because the water will expand as it turns
to ice and crack the glass.

Rabbits need bulk
so make sure they get hay as well as root
vegetables, green food and mixed cereals.

Hay is an essential part of a rabbit's diet
because it provides roughage. Apple tree
twigs are also a good source of roughage.

Don't suddenly change your rabbit's diet;
the bacteria in their stomach which
break down their food needs time to
adapt to any changes.

**Rabbits produce two kinds of droppings –
the good and the bad!**
The first sort is made up of partially
digested food and is usually passed at

night. These droppings are full of
nutrients which the rabbit eats so that
they are absorbed into its small intestine.
The other kind are large, round and stay
on the ground!

If your rabbit develops diarrhoea,
give it a weed called shepherd's purse
which should help its condition.

Don't let rabbits graze where dogs have been.
They could pick up tapeworm.

Rabbits are able to suck in their cheeks
when they eat which stops sharp, tough
things like twigs from getting into their
mouths.

Make nail clipping easy.
Rabbits are pushovers when it comes to
putting them in a trance. Simply lie your
rabbit on his back and gently stroke his
tummy until he drifts off. You can then
clip his nails without fuss before
snapping your fingers and bringing him
back to the real world!

Handle your rabbit frequently
 so that he gets used to it. Always be
 gentle. Pick the rabbit up with both
 hands, placed just behind the front legs.
 Don't pick a rabbit up by the ears or the
 scruff of its neck.

If a rabbit panics while you are holding it,
 put it down on the floor. Rabbits have
 powerful hind legs and you could get
 badly scratched trying to restrain it.

Placing your hand round its ears
 will help calm a struggling rabbit.

Don't pick up a rabbit with your bare arms
 because you could get badly scratched.

**If your rabbit starts circling your feet and
biting your ankles,**
 it could be sexually frustrated. Neutering
 can reduce aggressive behaviour.

Rabbits are territorial.

When you open the cage, let them come out on their own; don't reach in and drag them out because they could bite you.

If your rabbit gives you a nip,

let out a sudden high-pitched, loud screech to let him know he hurt you. Keep on squealing every time you are nipped; soon, your rabbit will get the message and be more gentle.

Put ice

on the spot where your rabbit has nipped you to ease the pain.

Rabbits like to climb.

Put shelves in their hutch.

If the hutch is to be kept outside

make sure it's in a sheltered, draught-free area.

You can put your rabbit's hutch on an overgrown patch of your vegetable garden.

They'll help to keep the weeds down and their droppings will fertilize the earth.

Netherland dwarf rabbits can be martyrs to their teeth

because sometimes their teeth don't fit together properly which makes eating difficult.

Give your rabbit something to gnaw on

like a log or piece of hard baked bread. It's better they chew away on something like this rather than their cage.

Lop rabbits have extremely long ears

which can grow to over 24 in/60 cm long. The Dwarf Lop makes a good pet because it doesn't need any special care and has a nice, friendly nature.

Angora rabbits

are one of the oldest breeds and can look spectacular but they do need a lot of grooming and special housing.

Don't keep buck rabbits together in a cage

because they will probably fight each other all the time.

If you keep doe rabbits together,
> they will often experience false
> pregnancies.

A pregnant rabbit
> pulls at its fur to make a soft nest for
> its young.

If you want to breed from your rabbits,
> put a doe and buck together! Obvious
> really, isn't it? The female rabbit will
> immediately start to produce eggs once
> she is placed with a male. Rabbits are
> pregnant for around 31 days.

Rabbits can be house-trained
> – you can teach them to use a litter tray.
> Unlike cats, they don't damage the
> furniture, but can scratch the carpet.

Clean litterboxes often
> to encourage a rabbit to use them. Rabbit
> wee is really smelly so you won't want to
> leave used litter hanging around.

If your rabbit has an accident on the carpet,
clean the stain with white vinegar or
soda water.

If you let your rabbit in your house,
don't encourage it to climb the stairs.
If it falls, it could damage its back badly.

Guinea Pigs

....

'If you lift a guinea pig up by the tail
His eyes drop out.'
Frederick Locker-Lampson

**Guinea pigs are partial to left-over cooked
peas.**

Treat your guinea pig
– give him some toast.

**Recycle your guinea pig's droppings and
left-over food.**
Sprinkle them on the garden to grow
sprouted oats which, when peeled, can
be fed back to him.

Give your guinea pigs hay all year round.
> The floor of the cage should be covered
> in it.

**Guinea pigs' mouths are right underneath
their heads**
> which means that they have to feed from
> the floor, so don't leave their food where
> they can't reach it.

Don't leave uneaten food in the cage
> because it will quickly go off.

Guinea pigs can't 'make' Vitamin C
> so you must ensure that their diet
> includes Vitamin C-rich food (broccoli,
> carrots, swede or any dark green leafy
> vegetable).

Spinach leaves
> drive guinea pigs wild.

**Avoid feeding your guinea pig rhubarb and
beetroot leaves**
> because these are poisonous.

Lettuce leaves have a high water content
> so aren't very nutritious.

Guinea pigs love
> melon, tomato and weeds.

If you like the grunts and squeals that guinea pigs make,
> start to make a regular noise just before you feed your pets. Like Pavlov's dog, they'll start squeaking themselves into a frenzy.

If your guinea pig starts to rumble
> it means that he's not happy.

A happy guinea pig
> is a leaping guinea pig.

You can keep male (buck) guinea pigs together,
> so long as they are introduced to the cage at the same time.

Stop males from fighting.
Put a few drops of neat lavender oil on
their bottoms. It confuses their sense
of smell.

Guinea pig females are pregnant
for around 63 days. Avoid handling a
pregnant female because you could
damage her unborn babies.

When guinea pigs are born
they are the spitting image of their
parents – a full coat and open eyes.

Get your guinea pig used to being handled
– support the whole body when you lift
him up and hold onto him with the other
hand so he doesn't make a dash for
freedom and end up injuring himself.

When trimming a guinea pig's toenails,
put him on a tennis racket. His toenails
will poke down through the gaps of the
strings, making them easier to clip.
Avoid cutting into the quick.

One way to avoid clipping toenails

is to give your guinea pigs a hard,
abrasive surface to walk on so that their
nails wear down naturally. Bricks,
without holes in them, are the cheapest
and easiest solution.

Guinea pigs can be very chatty

and have a full range of sounds. Try not
to alarm them (for example by picking
them up unexpectedly) because they
tend to shriek at full volume!

**It's not a good idea to give your guinea pig
the run of the house**

because it's all too easy to lose him
behind the furniture. If you really want
to have him indoors, build him an indoor
run.

If you've just laid a new lawn,

give it a chance to settle down first
before introducing your pets onto it.
New grass is often treated with weed
killer which can harm animals.

You can keep a guinea pig in with a rabbit
– they seem to get on rather well.

Guinea pigs have been farmed for fur and food
for over 2,500 years in South America.

Another name for a guinea pig
is a cavie.

Not too hot, not too cold.
Guinea pigs can cope with cold more
than heat so don't put their cages too
near radiators or hot-water pipes.

Make sure the cage is sheltered
from the sun.

While guinea pigs aren't rocket scientists, they're not stupid either.
They can be trained to use a litter tray
when out of the cage and will come
when called. Training takes time but the
potential is there.

Unwelcome Visitors

....

Human hair deters the most determined rabbit
from nibbling garden plants. If you're a
bit thin on top due to the stress for your
unwelcome visitors, ask a barber or
hairdresser for cuttings to sprinkle round
the base of the plants.

Leave your rose pruning on the ground;
rabbits (and cats for that matter) don't
like a prickly surface.

RATS, MICE, HAMSTERS AND GERBILS

....

'The trouble with the rat race is that
even if you win, you're still a rat.'
Lily Tomlin

These pets are ideal for the novice 'keeper'.

You should allow at least half an hour each day

for your pet, even more if you only have one animal.

When choosing a pet,

look for a healthy animal. There shouldn't be any bald patches on their fur and they should be alert and agile. Small scars on ears and tails are not necessarily signs of illness but are probably from old fights.

Always try to choose a young rodent as a pet

because these animals tend to have quite a short life span. A young mouse or rat can be taken from its mother when it's four weeks of age.

During the summer months,

drinking bottles for small animals often get covered in green algae. To get rid of it, fill the bottle with sand and water, shake it vigorously and rinse it out thoroughly. The sand scours the algae off the glass.

To clean a small-necked water bottle,
> fill it with a little water and a plug chain.
> Rattle it round for a bit until the stains
> come off the inside.

Stop water bottles from freezing
> by adding a few drops of glycerine to the
> water.

To get into awkward nooks and crannies when cleaning the cage,
> use an old toothbrush. It's a great tool.

Position the cage in a slightly raised position.
> Mice and rats react strongly to danger
> from above even if it's only you coming
> to feed them. Eye level is about right.

Try to put the cage in a busy area.
> Rats and mice love to see, smell and hear
> what's going on.

When picking up a rodent,
> try not to swoop down from above in
> case you frighten your pet. Allow them
> to sniff your hand before you pick
> them up.

Keep flies out of cages
- hang old net curtains over the front
of the cage.

Rats and Mice

....

*'When the mouse laughs at the cat, there
is a hole nearby.'*
Nigerian proverb

To lure a rat out from under the furniture,
entice him (or her) by holding a rat of
the opposite sex a short distance away.

Alternatively,
if your mouse or rat gets out, put a
cardboard tube on the floor with some
food inside it. Once it runs inside, close
both ends with your hands and return
the escapee to its cage.

Rats like sleeping in old shoe boxes
- or three-litre wine boxes (with the wine
bag removed, of course!).

Rats can be kept in guinea-pig cages

because they can't slip through the bars.

If you're worried about your pet mice escaping from a wire cage,

see whether you can get your finger through the wire. If you can, a young mouse can get out.

The advantage of wire cages

is that mice love to climb and the wire gives them ample opportunity to do this.

Don't keep rats and mice together.

Wood shavings are ideal as litter.

They are very absorbent and cheap to buy. Spread them around the cage, about 1½ in/4 cm thick. Don't use cedar or pine though because they contain toxins.

Rats and mice tend to use the corners of the cage as their toilet.

You could try adding a layer of cat litter in their favourite spots. It will help keep the smell down too.

Female mice don't have the same musky odour
as male mice.

Mice like their cages to smell familiar.
Try changing only half the litter at a time so a familiar smell remains.

Equally,
put back a little bit of old bedding each time you clean the cage so that there is a familiar smell where the mice sleep too.

A cheap alternative to rat food
is out-of-date baby food.

Rat delicacies also include
titbits such as biscuits (both human and dog varieties), apples and tomatoes. But remember to keep your rats on a balanced diet.

Try to avoid feeding too many berries to your rodents
as this can cause them to wee more often and make their litter really damp.

Avoid windy pets

– don't give them cabbage and onions.

Rats don't fight as much as mice

so you can keep rats together more easily. Adult male mice tend to be argumentative with each other so are best kept apart.

You can keep mice and rats on their own as individuals

but you will have to give them a lot of love and attention to make up for lack of rodent companions.

Rats can be taught to come when you call their name.

Mice are sexually mature

at 30–49 days old while rats can wait a little longer – 30–79 days!

Pick up rats by their shoulders

with your thumb held under their chin to stop them from biting. Don't pick a rat up by the scruff of its neck – it'll take a lump out of your finger for thanks.

Mice can be picked up
by the scruff of their neck.

Equally,
grasp the base of a mouse's tail firmly
and lift its hindquarters. Slide your other
hand under its bottom and then lift your
hand with the mouse sitting on it.

Keep your rats or mice amused
– fill their cages with cardboard tubes,
climbing frames, ladders and exercise
wheels. Don't have anything made of
plastic though; it will get gnawed to
bits and could damage your pet's insides.

Give mice a challenge
– don't make life too easy for them. If
you're about to feed your mice, put the
food on a different level so they have to
climb up to it. Make ladders steeper or
give them ropes as bridges.

Mice love empty eggboxes
– they're great to chew to pieces.

Rats love to gnaw on things.
> Try rawhide chew sticks or dog biscuits.

Alternatively,
> cooked soup bones are a particular ratty favourite.

Avocado
> goes down a treat with a rat.

Mice adore sunflower seeds
> but don't give a fat mouse this kind of treat.

To help a mouse lose weight,
> cut out oily seeds (like sunflower seeds or peanuts) and fatty treats. Give it soaked stale bread or plain boiled wholegrain rice with fruit and vegetables.

Cheese is not an ideal treat for a mouse
> because mice don't feed on dairy products in the wild. Cheese is, however, a convenient way to bait mousetraps!

Rats and mice can be fed a few treats now and again.

Dry, healthy, low-sugar cereals, plain popcorn, dry oatmeal, spaghetti or wild bird seed all add variety to their diet.

A rat will require a wheel

that is at least 12–14 in/30–35 cm in diameter.

A cheap but effective toy for mice

is a section of branch with holes bored into it. Your mice can use it as a climbing frame and ladder.

Alternatively,

an upside-down terracotta flower pot with holes in the edge makes an ideal hidey hole for mice or rats.

Add a few small branches from a birch, beech tree or hazel bush.

It will give your rat or mouse something to clamber up and down and explore from.

Hamsters

....

Hamsters are very active at night.
    If you want a good night's sleep, don't
    keep their cage in the bedroom with you.

When buying a hamster,
    try to do so in the evening because it will
    be more active.

A healthy hamster
    should have a smooth, well-rounded
    body, with no bald patches on the coat.
    The eyes should be bright and clear. The
    ears should be clean and, if you're buying
    a young hamster, should have hair on the
    outside.

Male and female hamsters
    are equally good tempered.

You can keep two hamsters in one cage
    depending on what kind you want to get.
    Short dwarf hamsters and Russian
    hamsters are sociable souls and will live

together. But it's best if they've been together since birth and are of the same sex. All other hamsters should be kept separately because they are territorial.

When waking your hamster,

make noises, talk to him gently, and move the cage to and fro so he's not rudely awakened and becomes frightened.

Hamsters are great swingers.

Slip a piece of string through the length of a cardboard tube, knot the ends and hang from the top of their cage to make a fun swing for them.

To clean their cage,

half fill a jam jar with sawdust, put it on its side and encourage the hamsters to explore it while you do the housework on the cage. A jam jar filled with sawdust also works as a hamster loo in one corner of the cage.

Baby hamsters

love porridge and similar cereals.

Feed your hamster once a day,
>   in the late afternoon or evening.

An adult hamster eats only a tablespoon of food
>   or less a day.

Avoid iceberg lettuce and citrus fruits.
>   Give small amounts of juicy fruits, like tomatoes, strawberries or pears.

Hamsters are rather partial to yoghurt
>   but don't give them a rich variety like chocolate or caramel. They should eat no more than a teaspoon of yoghurt two or three times a week as a treat.

Teach your baby hamster to like being handled
>   by always feeding him straight after playtime.

To prevent your hamster from going into a state of hibernation,
>   warm him up gently in your hands... not by the fire.

If your hamster bites,
use a small fishing net to catch him and
save your fingers from nips.

To stop hamsters from biting
scoop them up from below when you
want to pick them up. If you pick them
up from above, they think they're being
attacked and become aggressive.

If your hamster does bite you,
put him back in the cage and leave him
for a couple of hours so he can calm
down.

To groom your long-haired hamster,
use an old comb or toothbrush.

Give a hamster something to play with
– cotton reels, jars… anything as long as
it hasn't got sharp edges and isn't likely
to be toxic.

Give your hamster something to chew on
– attach some white wood to the side of
the cage. Alternatively, use a clothes peg.

Don't use cotton wool or anything similar as bedding

because it can be dangerous if eaten.

To help your hamster get over a cold,

feed him a mixture of lukewarm milk, water and a drop of honey.

If your hamster escapes,

try leaving some sunflower seeds in each room of the house. Shut all the doors and go to bed. The next morning, you'll be able to tell which room he's ended up in by the absence of seeds. Once you know which rooms he's in, get his cage and leave it with the door open and food inside.

Alternatively,

put a pile of food in the centre of the floor and surround it with a ring of flour. Then just follow the footprints till you find the escapee.

If your hamster escapes,

put some food in the bottom of a bucket and lean a small, hamster-sized ramp up the side. The hamster will smell the food, go and investigate and drop to the bottom of the bucket with no means of getting out again (this works for mice too).

Gerbils

When buying a gerbil,
look for an animal that is bright eyed, alert and inquisitive. If it's dozy and disinterested, it could be ill.

Gerbils are very gregarious
and hate to be kept on their own. Two same sex pairs will bond as closely as a mated pair and be as happy as Larry.

Gerbils make ideal pets
because they are desert animals. This means that they make very efficient use of food and water and hardly wee at all! That means you don't have to clean their cages as much as other rodent pets.

If you want to restrain a gerbil

– hold it firmly by the base of the tail.
Try to avoid grabbing the tail any further
towards the tip because you could
damage it.

Wooden cages are hard to keep clean.

Gerbils also tend to chew large bits off
so stick to a metal cage.

**However, give them a bit of wood or a branch
to gnaw**

and it will also serve as a lookout point
for inquisitive pets and help the cage
look attractive.

As desert creatures,

gerbils are used to dry conditions and
like to dig. Give them plenty of wood
shavings (about 2 in/5 cm deep) to
burrow in.

Put a dish full of sand in your gerbil's cage;

they love to have sandbaths. It helps to
keep their fur in good condition. Change
the sand every few days.

Hay is much appreciated

as a nest-building material.

A gerbil's idea of a des. res.

is an old coconut shell. It may not be
much to you or me but it's a palace to
him. Place it in his cage.

Don't get your gerbil a hamster wheel to play with.

He might catch his tail in the open
spaces.

Stop sawdust from getting everywhere.

Cut the sides of a cardboard box down
to 1 in/2.5 cm and stand the hutch in it.
The sawdust collects in the bottom of
the box and can be shaken out every few
days.

Unlike many animals, gerbils practise a form of birth control.

If you have a breeding pair that produces
a litter or two then they won't have any
more. If, however, you remove the litter,
the parents become fertile again.

Gerbils are sexually mature
    at 60–80 days.

Gerbils are unusual in that they generally mate for life
    in pairs (or sometimes as a threesome, the kinky devils).

Unwelcome Visitors

....

'In baiting a mouse-trap with cheese, always leave room for the mouse.'
Saki

You think you've got mice but you're not sure?
    Sprinkle flour where you believe them to be and next morning check it for footprints. If you're lucky you can then track them to their hole.

Block up small holes to keep mice out.

Mice can squeeze through the tiniest hole. If you can fit a pen through a space then it's big enough for a mouse.

Deter mice from entering your home

by attaching a bristle strip to doorways.

Attract mice with their favourite titbits.

Mice prefer fruit and nut chocolate to cheese – unless they live in Birmingham where the local rodent population have a yen for tuna (I kid you not; an earnest postgraduate student spent two years studying the phenomenon).

A humane way to catch a mouse

is to use a wide-necked jar. Fill the bottom with broken chocolate biscuits (unless you're in Birmingham) and lean a ramp against the jar. The mouse will climb in but won't be able to get out. You can then release him outside.

A refreshing way to evict a mouse

is to squirt minty toothpaste around
the edges of its hole. Mice don't like the
smell.

Double your chances of catching a mouse

by placing the trap at right angles to the
wall. Mice feel insecure in the middle of
a room and are more likely to skirt the
edges.

REPTILES AND AMPHIBIANS

....

'There's a snake hidden in the grass.'
Virgil

If you're going to buy a snake,

take a pillow case with you to the shop
or breeder. You can then wrap the snake
in it so that it won't become too stressed
while you take it home with you.

If your reptile gets a cold,

put a jar of vapour rub in its cage and
turn the heat up.

Snakes don't require a lot of space.

A cage one half to two thirds of its body
length is sufficient for most adult snakes.

Snakes are shy creatures

so give them somewhere to hide; a
cardboard box, turned upside down with
a hole cut in the side is perfectly
adequate.

Don't feed your new snake when you get it home.

Give it a few days to settle down and get
used to its surroundings.

Temperature is extremely important;

the cage should be kept at a temperature
of between 80–86°F/28–30°C with an
incandescent red light (red bulbs cause
less stress to snakes). Don't guess at the
temperature – use a thermometer.

Proper lighting is important

for reptiles because it aids in calcium
metabolism. You need the full source of
spectrum lighting that provides UVA and
UVB rays.

To handle a lizard properly,

pick it up by holding it firmly around its
body and forelegs – never by the tail.

**Most reptiles and amphibians become less
active when they are cold.**

This makes them easier to handle.
Put them in the fridge for a short while
(in a container, of course). On no account
try to speed up the process by using the
freezer. Don't leave them in the fridge for
longer than a few minutes. If ice crystals
form on their bodies it can cause a lot of
pain and distress.

To help a lizard adapt to its surroundings,
cover the floor with enough sand and
gravel for it to bury itself.

To create a perfect basking area,
place a rock inside the vivarium.

Margarine pots
are excellent wet boxes for geckos.

Snakes eat other animals
– when thinking about buying a snake
as a pet, it's worth investigating whether
you will have a ready supply of rats and
mice.

**Young snakes will need to eat about once a
week.**
Adult snakes can be fed twice a month.
For really large snakes, such as boas and
pythons, you need only feed them once
a month.

When feeding a snake defrosted mice,
warm food with a hair-drier for a while.
This will make it look and smell more
like the real thing.

Never put frozen rats or mice in the microwave

because it will build up with bacteria. Allow them to defrost naturally. Feed them whole for roughage.

Don't leave live food animals in with your snake;

mice and rats can give a nasty bite that can seriously injure a reptile.

If your snake is having problems eating,

feed it at night or when you have turned off all the lights. This will make it feel more secure and it should go back to its normal routine. If the problem persists, take it to the vet.

When feeding a snake with tweezers,

ensure that you wrap rubber bits round the end of your tweezers so you don't damage its teeth or mouth.

Don't handle a snake immediately after feeding.

It will be sick. Leave it for a day or two.

If your snake has difficulty shedding its skin,
get a good dollop of vegetable oil on your hands and stroke the snake from head to tail. You should find that the skin will come off more easily then.

If there's a problem shedding skin from around the eye area,
wrap a bit of masking tape round your finger and gently remove the skin with this.

If your snake is laying eggs,
she'll appreciate a good hide. Drape a towel over two pieces of wood and she'll curl up underneath. Spray the towel regularly to maintain humidity.

Use old egg boxes
for your snake's favourite dish – crickets – to jump around in.

Bearded dragons make good pets
– they can be extremely tame but have high energy levels and big appetites with personalities to match.

The more you handle a bearded dragon,
the tamer it will become. Soon, you
will have them eating out of your hand
(literally!) and perching on your shoulder
quite happily.

**Bearded dragons need a light source for
basking and the daily heating of their bodies.**
You will also need to provide places to
hide so that they can regulate their body
temperature.

**If you don't want a large lizard, don't get a
green iguana.**
Properly cared for, they can reach 5–6 ft/
1.5–1.8 m within four to five years.

**Green iguanas can live for up to 20 years
in captivity**
and weigh up to 18 lb/8 kg.

**In the wild, iguanas feel more comfortable
in trees.**
Make sure you have enough height in
their tank to allow them to climb.

Iguanas love to climb

so provide them with branches, ropes
or towels to climb up and bask on. Make
sure they are securely placed to prevent
your pet from falling.

Choosing a suitable flooring (or substrate) for your iguana's cage is important.

Artificial grass, carpet or paper towels
are ideal. Always have a few pieces in
reserve so that while a soiled piece is
being washed and disinfected, you can
put the spare pieces in the tank. The
clean piece must be completely dry
before you replace it.

Newspaper does not make suitable flooring for iguanas

because the ink can get into their skin.

Iguanas don't need to eat meat;

they can be raised on a strictly plant-
based diet, getting their protein from
plant materials. Alfalfa is an excellent
source of plant protein.

Chop your iguana food carefully.

Although they have a sharp set of teeth,
iguanas don't chew their food – they gulp
it down. So don't give them big pieces.

**You can make up a week's worth of basic
salad for your lizard**

and keep it in an airtight container in the
fridge. Just spoon in the required amount
when you need to. A good mix would
consist of green beans, alfalfa, parsnip
and fruit.

Add a little extra to your iguana's salad

with some left-overs. A bit of rice or
bread will add extra calcium to their diet.

To house an aquatic amphibian,

you need the water to be at least 6 in/
15 cm deep for the animal to swim in.
So make sure you've got a good water
filtration system.

To distinguish toads from frogs

– check their skin. A toad has a dry,
warty skin, shorter hind legs and a flatter
appearance.

To keep your frogs happy,

collect moss from trees, wash it and put in with the frogs. Then spray it regularly to keep it damp.

Frogs eat slugs and snails

– they make up about 25 per cent of their diet.

You can't get warts from a frog

– that's just an old wives' tale.

A group of frogs is called

an 'army' of frogs. And a group of toads is called a 'knot' of toads.

When a frog swallows, his eyeballs go down into his head.

This is because the eyeballs apply pressure and help push the food down the frog's throat.

Toads are partial to

ants, beetles and woodlice. Earthworms always go down well.

To ensure your newts enjoy a nutritious diet,
give them earthworms, tadpoles and
insect larvae... don't give them anything
that moves too quickly.

If you have to handle an amphibian
(such as a frog, toad, newt or
salamander), make sure your hands are
slightly damp. They have very sensitive
skin.

Never mix different species together
– many amphibians can secrete toxins
that can be deadly to other species.

**Always wash your hands after handling your
pet.**

Grass snakes are harmless to humans
– their only form of defence is to play
dead.

Slow worms are not snakes,
they are lizards, so don't handle them by
the tail. They are usually extremely
friendly and happy to be handled.

Slow worms eat in the late afternoon or early evening.

Give them snails, slugs, worms and insects.

If you are bitten by a venomous snake,

forget what you saw in the old Western movies. Don't try and suck the poison out with your mouth or try to cut into the bite. Let the bite bleed freely for 15–30 seconds. Cleanse and disinfect the area quickly with iodine. Apply hard direct pressure over the bite and tape an adhesive bandage in place (tightly, as if it were a sprain). Then get to a hospital as quickly as possible.

If you come across a snake in the field and don't know what it is,

don't approach it, try to examine it or take a photo (unless you've got a zoom lens).

WILD THINGS

······································

'*Of all the animals, man is the only one that is cruel. He is the only one that inflicts pain for the pleasure of doing it.*'
Mark Twain

To attract wild life to your land

plant mountain ash or alder. They are fast-growing trees and produce lots of fruit for the birds.

In the spring, you may come across a baby animal.

Don't assume it's been abandoned – just leave it alone. Unless it's obviously hurt or in danger, retreat to a discreet distance and keep an eye on it if you're not sure whether the parents are around.

Squirrels

Squirrels hate loud noise

so try playing heavy metal music at full volume. The neighbours will hate it but, more importantly, so will the squirrels.

Keep squirrels and birds out of roof eaves and rafters

by screwing chicken wire into tight balls and pushing it into any awkward holes or crannies.

Unlike many wild animals, a squirrel does not like being enclosed in a box.

So if you have caught an injured one and intend to take it to a vet, use a cage instead. Make sure it's made from metal – squirrels have sharp teeth.

If you are tending to an injured red squirrel,

you will have to contact your local Nature Conservancy Council. They are a protected species and you will need a licence to care for one.

Foxes

Keep foxes out of the garden

by spreading lion dung around the edges.
You don't have to gather your own lion
poo; just ask at the local zoo for a batch.

Stop foxes from eating your pheasants.

Place mirrors or plastic bags round the
pen and it should help to deter them.

If you are looking after an injured fox,

give some thought to its water container.
Foxes love peeing in them so you will
have to come up with a more suitable
alternative.

To feed a fox cub,

don't use cow's milk. Feed them goat's
milk every three or four hours. You'll
need to use a bottle if the cubs are less
than four weeks old. They can go onto
solids when they are about a month old.

Moles

Moles hate any foul smelling liquid
– try pouring cleaning fluid or old flower water around the entrance to mole hills.

Alternatively,
alarm them into leaving. Set an alarm clock and shove it down the mole hole. Once it goes off, the moles should leave home.

Sink empty bottles up to their necks
in the garden. Moles don't like the sound of the wind across the empty tops.

Stick a child's windmill in the ground
near a mole's run. It causes vibrations to run down the stem and into the run which disturbs the mole.

Deter moles
by lining the bottom of their run with gorse. Moles hate having their noses pricked.

Hedgehogs

....

If you have to catch a hedgehog but don't want to handle it,

wait till it's rolled into a ball and then gently roll it onto a handkerchief or piece of newspaper which you can use to transport it.

If you want a hedgehog to unroll so you can examine it,

hold it in the palm of your hand and gently rock it backwards and forwards. The theory is that the animal will get a bit giddy and will unroll to see what on earth's going on.

Alternatively,

try and work out where the head is and hold it pointing downwards over a table. The hedgehog should start to unroll and try to reach the surface below. You can then hold it gently by its hind legs.

Hedgehogs are nocturnal animals

so if you find one during the day there must be something wrong with it.

Hedgehogs drink a lot of water;
> they will need up to 4 fl oz/120 ml at
> a time.

Don't feed milk to hedgehogs
> – water is best.

Hedgehogs are the gardener's friend.
> They will quite happily keep the slug
> and beetle populations down for you.

**If you're keen to leave food out for a
hedgehog,**
> try pet foods and baby foods, not milk
> and water.

If you need to force feed a sick hedgehog,
> dribble a solution of warm water and
> glucose into its mouth with a syringe.

**Baby hedgehogs with their eyes closed need
to be fed every two to three hours;**
> they will need about ½ teaspoon of milk
> and water with a dash of glucose.

If you don't have a pipette for feeding,

you could try a paint brush or small spoon.

After each feed,

a baby hedgehog must be cleaned and gently massaged with baby oil or kitchen wipes. You have to imitate the licking action of the mother which stimulates circulation.

Equally, you need to encourage a baby to empty its bowels.

Dip a cotton bud in warm water and gently tickle the baby's bottom. Do this before and after each feed.

You must keep a baby or injured hedgehog warm.

Wrap a hot water bottle in an old jumper and put it in the bottom of a cardboard box with the hedgehog.

Don't release a hedgehog into the wild
until it weighs 1 lb 6 oz/625 g. Wait for
warmer weather (around April time in
Britain) because there will be plenty of
insects around for him to eat.

**Try to release a hedgehog where there are
other hedgehogs.**
This means that there is enough food and
shelter for them to survive.

Hedgehogs love garden bonfire heaps;
they make ideal places to hibernate.
Always turn your bonfire over to check
for guests before setting it alight.

**Secure a piece of chicken wire so that it
dangles into your garden pond or swimming
pool.**
Hedgehogs can swim but might need
some help getting out again.

**Always check grass and weeds before using
a strimmer**
because these are ideal places to nest
if you're a hedgehog.

The gap underneath a raised shed provides excellent shelter for hedgehogs

and keeps them out of the clutches of any cats.

Deer

....

One way to keep deer away

is to hang bars of soap around your crops or garden.

If you accidentally corner a female deer

watch out for its front feet. They are great boxers when they need to be and often use their feet first rather than their horns.

Avoid deer during the rut season, especially male deer.

A fully antlered red stag in rut is quite capable of disembowelling a person.

When caring for an injured deer that doesn't want to eat,

it's worth persevering with force feeding. Make up some baby cereal so that it's very thick and squeeze or dribble it into its mouth. A pint/600 ml, two or three times a day, for a large deer will do the trick.

When feeding a fawn,

give it goat's milk in a baby's feeding bottle. You could mix in some cod liver oil or egg as well.

Bats

If you have to handle a bat,

be careful not to hold its wings because they are extremely fragile. Support its body. Better still, offer it a vertical surface and it will instinctively turn itself upside down and hang downwards, gripping with its hind feet.

During the day, bats become torpid

so won't react if you go near them.
After resting, they have to raise their
body temperature which they do by
shivering for around half an hour before
they can fly.

**If you find a bat crawling around the house
or garden in the summer,**

it's likely to be a baby. Pop it in a
ventilated box until dusk and then
hang the open box outside near the
roost where its mother can get at it.

**An injured bat will need water as soon
as possible;**

use an eye dropper or syringe.

If you are looking after a baby bat,

feed it skimmed milk through a syringe.

Ferrets

Ferrets have a nasty bite.

If you're unfortunate enough to be on the receiving end of its teeth, try to let the animal's feet rest on the ground (even though your instinct will be to pull away from the source of pain). Once it feels its feet on solid ground, it will probably be so pleased it will let you go.

If your ferret still hangs on grimly,

try pinching its forehead or a foot to distract it.

Most ferrets are easy to handle, however.

Just support its body with your hand. Putting your thumb under its chin means it won't be tempted to bite you.

If you want to catch a ferret, try using a tube.

They are incredibly curious and love dark holes to explore. A piece of drainpipe with the cage at the other end is one way to catch them.

Wild Birds

....

'A Robin Redbreast in a Cage
Puts all Heaven in a Rage.'
William Blake

To make your own instant bird feeder,

take the cardboard tube from a loo roll
or kitchen paper roll and cover it in
honey. Then roll it over some bird seed
until it's completely covered. You can
then hang it outside and enjoy watching
the birds as they eat.

Prevent birds from eating window putty

– they're after the linseed oil – by mixing
black pepper into the putty.

Fences provide the ideal site for bird boxes

or standing posts for birds of prey. Just
put in the occasional tall pole and fix a
bird box or perch on to the pole.

Give the birds a treat

– place small piles of wood and branches around your land. These 'islands' will soon fill up with insects, providing a welcome source of food for the birds.

To make an instant birdbath,

turn a frisbee upside down. Stick some wire through opposite edges and you can hang it from a tree.

To avoid disturbing birds that may be nesting

around your pond, only mow towards the end of August.

If a goose tries to attack you,

call its bluff and advance towards it rather than retreat. It will usually turn tail and run, unless it's protecting a nest.

To transport a bird such as a swan or goose,

chop the corner off an old sack and pop it over the bird. They can put their head through the hole but their wings and body are kept secure.

When handling birds such as ravens or herons,

keep an eye on their beaks which are formidable weapons. If you have to examine them, slip a rubber band over the end of the beak for your safety. Don't leave it there for very long.

When handling birds of prey,

wear heavy-duty gloves. Their beaks and claws are designed for ripping and tearing. They should be handled by experts but if you're in a position where you have to catch one, don't handle it more than necessary. Put it in a warm, dark, ventilated box (not a cage) until you can hand it over to an expert.

With birds of prey, a hooded bird is a quiet bird.

An old sock, with a hole for the beak, will be an effective hood. Don't try hooding an owl, however... it won't work!

Don't bind the beak of a bird while transporting it

because it may want to throw up as a result of the stress of the capture.

When feeding birds of prey

who might not be used to dead food, try cutting up a day-old chick so that its innards are exposed.

Pot-Bellied Pigs

....

'I like pigs. Dogs look up to us. Cats look down on us. Pigs treat us as equals.'
Winston Churchill

Why get a dog?

Pot-bellied pigs are intelligent and can be trained as you would a dog. They respond to litter training, can do simple tricks and walk on a lead.

Pot-bellied pigs can be kept indoors or outdoors.

Give them some shelter if they are kept outside.

In hot spells,

they will need a pool of water to keep cool.

Even domesticated pigs need to root around

so make sure they have an area of soft dirt or soil to stick their snout in.

Puberty hits in at around six or seven months of age.

If you don't plan to breed from your pigs, you can have them spayed or neutered at around three to four months old.

If your pig does have a litter,

the piglets' needle teeth should be trimmed so that the sow and other piglets don't get nipped by the sharp teeth.

Pot-bellied pigs aren't aggressive

but they can give a nasty nip if their canine teeth aren't removed. You can have them removed when the pig is around four months old.

These pigs don't raise a stink.

In fact, they hardly pong at all.

Grooming is important.

Brush them down with a soft bristle brush each day. Hooves and tusks will need trimming regularly.

Down On the Farm

'The cow is of the bovine ilk,
One end is moo, the other, milk.'
Ogden Nash

Owls can be fatally attracted to water troughs

so float a piece of wood on the surface. This will allow the bird to get itself out of danger.

To keep your cattle troughs clear
>   put goldfish in them.

If you are worried about hedgehogs getting trapped in cattle grids,
>   put a brick or little ramp on the inside
>   so that they have an escape route.

For the optimum shelter for your animals,
>   keep your hedges at a minimum
>   6.5 ft/2 m high.

Ensure that your hedges are stocked with fruits
>   for birds and mammals – trim the hedges
>   in winter.

Keep your ducks happy
>   while they're moulting. They can't fly
>   at this time so check on them regularly
>   during the summer.

If you are worried that a fox might eat your duck eggs,
>   don't go looking for the nest. Your scent
>   will lead the fox straight to the clutch
>   of eggs.

Never trust a bull

even if you know him really well. Bulls
respond to dominant behaviour; twist
the nose ring slightly to let him know
who is boss.

To keep a cow from fidgeting,

hold her tail near the base and lift it up.
This will keep her still.

Always stand behind the head of a billy goat

to avoid being thumped.

Pigs are intelligent animals.

They respond well to being talked to,
quietly.

Only pick up a piglet if the sow is restrained.

Piglets tend to make an almighty row
when handled and this could alarm the
mother.

If you are shepherding sheep,

make sure that they can see an opening
in front of them. They hate entering dark
places, walking into their own shadows
or going into water.

Some sheep have a habit of falling over onto their back

and being unable to right themselves. If this happens, you must get them on their feet as soon as possible. They can get acute indigestion in this position and can even die.

Sheep have a blind spot so if you want to catch one, approach it from behind.

Sheep hate being on their own.

They're happiest in a group when they are much easier to handle.

Sheep are great ones for panicking.

If they are going to make a run for it, they tend to aim uphill or towards the light.

To examine a sheep, get it into a 'docile' position.

This involves it sitting on its back legs. One way to do this is to lift its front end then walk the sheep backwards until it sits down!

Exotica

....

*'Whenever you observe an animal closely,
you feel as if a human being sitting inside
were making fun of you.'*
Elias Canetti

If you run out of food in Arctic regions,

eat the dog food first and then the dogs.
(Dogs are now banned from the Antarctic
in case they infect the seals so don't run
out of food there.)

When you run out of food in the jungle,

don't eat any old insect you come across.
Insects protect themselves against
predators with warning colours. If they're
brightly coloured (such as red or yellow),
then you should avoid them because
they will probably be poisonous.

Always look before you touch

– danger comes from small creatures as
well as large. For example, scorpions seek
out dark places during the day so check
out your rucksack and boots carefully.

If you get stung by an insect,

> put some neat bleach on the afflicted area
> the ammonia will help to ease the pain.
> If you don't have any bleach, just have a
> pee and put the urine on the stung spot.

Llamas are intelligent

> and easy to train.

Become the best friend of weavers and knitters

> – give them llama hair to spin or knit
> into warm, luxurious garments!

If a llama spits at you,

> take notice. He's telling you to push off.

Generally, llamas are gentle and easy to get along with.

> They are extremely sociable and
> therefore shouldn't be kept on their own.

Llamas are multi-functional;

> they can carry heavy loads (up to 100 lb/
> 45 kg) and travel 12½–18½ miles/
> 20–30km a day. Some exclusive golf
> courses use them as caddies! They can

be trained to pull a cart and they make
great guard dogs (they're very territorial
and protective).

Thanks to their efficient digestive system,
llamas can polish off hay, grass, weeds,
shrubs and trees.

Worried about inquisitive polar bears?
Make your own early warning system.
Place ski poles around your camp site
and thread a string between them. Hang
anything that rattles or makes a noise on
the string.

To frighten off polar bears
shout as loud as you can and wave your
arms about. Look as big and aggressive
as possible!

**If you want to keep a monkey as a pet, be
warned**
– they can't be toilet trained.

Never keep a monkey on its own
– it needs companions of its own kind.

Capuchin monkeys like strong smells.
They have been known to rub food,
such as onions or orange peel, over their
bodies.

A cage can never be too strong for a monkey
– don't ever underestimate their ability
to escape.

Some monkeys scent mark their cage
so don't sterilize it when you clean it.
Always clean the nestbox and the cage
at different times so a familiar smell
remains at all times.

Gorillas are great bluffers
– all that rushing about and chest-beating
is usually just to try to scare intruders
away while the rest of the gorilla band
slope off quietly into the forest.

Gorillas and chimps love termites and ants
but hate getting bitten. So they slap the
ground to stun the insects before eating
them.

If you come across a beached whale or dolphin,

make sure its blowhole is clear so it can breathe. Try and keep it upright, and don't drag it by its tail. The skin should be kept cool and wet; you can use damp cloths and seaweed to cover it if necessary. Call the fire brigade for assistance.

Odds and Sods

When out camping or walking,

use an inverted frisbee as a water or food dish for your pet.

If an animal has suffered from a burn,

you must try to take the heat out of the affected area. Plunge the area into cold water for 10–15 minutes. Once the area is cool, you can cover it with a clean, dry bandage or cloth. Don't use oil or lotion.

Alternatively,

soak the cloth in very strong tea.
The tannin encourages the wound to
coagulate quickly and protect the
sensitive spot.

**If an animal has suffered burns caused by acid
or alkaline,**

remember that an acid substance will
neutralize an alkaline one and vice versa.
Milk or bicarbonate of soda (2 parts
bicarbonate to 98 parts water) to
neutralize acids; weak vinegar (5 parts
to 95 parts water) will neutralize alkalis
like caustic soda and ammonia.

**When an animal has swallowed something
acidic,**

neutralize the acid with alkaline
substances like bicarbonate of soda or
chalk (mixed in barley water or milk).
If you don't have anything alkaline to
hand, dilute the acid as much as possible
with water.

If you suspect an animal has eaten barbiturates,

give them an emetic and keep them warm. Even strong coffee will help.

Lead can be extremely dangerous to animals:

two pieces of lead shot can kill a pigeon. The best immediate treatment for mammals is a large dose of Epsom salts, milk, egg whites or strong tea. Send for the vet immediately and keep the animal warm and quiet.

Heatstroke is a killer

so you must do everything to cool the animal down as quickly as possible. Reduce body heat rapidly by showering with cold water, applying wet sheets and towels, putting paws in cold water and trying to get cold air into the lungs. Get the animal to a vet as soon as possible.

If an animal has eaten poison,

you need to give them an emetic to cause vomiting or a purgative to empty the bowels. Useful emetics are: salt with water (around 2 tablespoons to a cup), washing soda (about the size of a hazel

nut for a dog or cat), Epsom salts
or mustard in water (1 dessertspoon
in a cupful of water for a pig).

Animals can suffer from bee and wasp stings as well as humans.

If you can, remove the sting carefully.
Apply a paste of bicarbonate of soda to
the afflicted area.

Alternatively,

rub half a freshly cut onion over the sting
spot.

Tar can be difficult to get off fur (or skin, for that matter).

Use margarine, melted butter or
eucalyptus oil to remove it.

If creosote is the problem

wash it off as soon as possible using
warm soapy water or warm castor oil.
Make sure you clean the skin as well as
the fur.

If you are involved in a road traffic accident with horses, dogs or cattle,
> you have a legal obligation to report it to the police.

Give a stuffed animal a brilliant smile.
> Wipe its teeth with a wet wipe to whiten its fangs.

To spruce up a stuffed animal,
> sprinkle some baking soda over it. Leave for quarter of an hour and then carefully brush off.

To clean dark fur
> dry some bran in the oven, rub it into the fur and then cover with a warm blanket. You should leave it like this for half an hour before shaking the bran out and then brushing the fur.

To clean light fur
> rub some cornflour into the fur and roll it up in a warm blanket. Leave it like this for 24 hours before shaking out and brushing.

INDEX